Blacks in American Movies:

A Selected Bibliography

compiled and edited

by

ANNE POWERS

The Scarecrow Press, Inc.
Metuchen, N.J.   1974

Library of Congress Cataloging in Publication Data

Powers, Anne, 1947-
  Blacks in American movies.

    1. Negroes in the moving-picture industry--Bibliog-
raphy. I. Title.
Z5784.M9P69   016.79143'0973   74-19125
ISBN 0-8108-0753-X

for my mother
ROSALIE BYRD POWERS
and in loving memory of
my father
WILLIAM LLOYD POWERS

TABLE OF CONTENTS

List of Periodicals Cited   v

Preface   vii

Introduction   1

Non-Periodical References
    Indexes   7
    Bibliographies   8
    General Reference Works   9
    Dissertations   10
    Excerpts   11
    Extracts   12
    Books   13
    Biographies and Autobiographies   15

Subject Listing of Periodical Citations
    Summary of Contents   17
    The Listing   18

Alphabetical Periodical Listings   70

Chronological Listing   112

Filmography: Features By and About Blacks,
    1904-1930   142

Author and Subject Index   151

LIST OF PERIODICALS CITED

America
Black Creation
Black World
Box Office
Chicago Defender
Christian Century
Cinema
Cinemeditor
Collier's
Color
Commentary
Commonweal
Coronet
Crisis
Daily Variety
The Drama Review
Ebony
Encore
Entertainment World
Essence
Film Culture
Film Daily
Film Quarterly
Film-TV Daily
Films and Filming
Films in Review
Historian
Hollywood Citizen-News
Hollywood Reporter
Jet
Journal of Negro Education
Journal of Religious Thought
Journal of the Producer's
　Guild
Liberation
Liberator

Life
Literary Digest
Look
Los Angeles Daily News
Los Angeles Examiner
Los Angeles Herald Examiner
Los Angeles Sentinel
Los Angeles Times
Los Angeles Times Calendar
Massachusetts Review
Motion Picture Exhibitor
Motion Picture Herald
Movie/T.V. Marketing
National Review
Negro Digest
Negro History Bulletin
New Republic
New Masses
New York Tidings
New York Times
New York Times Magazine
New Yorker
Newsweek
Norfolk Journal and Guide
Opportunity
Our World
Phylon
Pittsburgh Courier
Political Science Quarterly
Quarterly of Film, Radio,
　& Television
Quick News Weekly
Reader's Digest
Saturday Review
Saturday Review of the Arts
Senior Scholastic

Sepia
Show
Sight and Sound
Social Problems
Soul Illustrated
Theatre Arts

Time
Tuesday Magazine
Variety Weekly
Vision
Wall Street Journal
Washington Post

PREFACE

The purpose of this bibliography is to provide students and other researchers with a listing of books, articles, and other material on Blacks in American films, and particularly to give them a much-needed guide to where to find periodical information on this subject.

The focus of this listing is on general commentary on Blacks in American films. The first part consists of a list of references, including general works, books, biographies, and other non-periodical listings. The material for the first periodical listing covers several distinct areas concerning Blacks in films, such as the "boom" in Black movies, individual Black actors and actresses, the position of the Black in the American cinema, etc.

This bibliography centers on the social significance of Black involvement in films, mostly within the American context. Also included are several articles dealing with Blacks in foreign-made films. Materials included have been chosen for their research value and pertinence to the subject; some works are annotated to clarify or pinpoint their thrust or form. Only English-language items have been included.

Periodical citations are listed alphabetically under various subject headings by title of article. Following the title of the article the name of the journal is given, then numbers indicating the journal's volume number, the page number(s), and finally the date. Explanatory phrases or sentences in parenthesis are added to some of the citations to clarify them where the compiler felt this was necessary.

> Example: "Hollywood director speaks out,"
> Negro Digest, 9:42-44, Jan. 51.
> (Jewish director Mark Robson talks
> about race in movies.)

The article title is followed by the name of the journal; the "9" designates Volume 9 of Negro Digest; the numbers "42-44" indicate the page numbers, and "Jan. 51" indicates the date of publication. The explanatory sentence identifies the Hollywood director and the topic which makes the article relevant to this bibliography. Newspaper citations give the name of the paper and the date.

Following the subject listings, two other features are presented. The first is a re-listing of the articles alphabetically by name of the journals and newspapers in which they appear; this is intended to aid those whose research is focused on where to find information on this subject, or on the point of view of a particular periodical in regard to Blacks in films, which may be inferred from the citations. The second feature is a chronological indexing of the articles for those who wish to trace the emphases of any particular period, from the 1920's to the present.

A filmography of features by and about Blacks up to 1930, and an author-subject index conclude the volume.

INTRODUCTION

The involvement of Blacks in American movies and the American theatre has been, in the seventies, the subject of much interest and controversy. Several works have appeared, or are scheduled to appear, that have attempted to appraise the value of Blacks' contributions to the acting arts. They offer insight and opinions of historical and sociological significance, and these become even more meaningful as we contemplate the apparently sudden upsurge of a host of successful Black films--a phenomenon whose background needs to be explored and explained.

The literature now available on this subject seems to be marked by a variety of "problems." There is "the Black Problem" itself, as represented in such American motion pictures as Pinky, Nothing But a Man, Imitation of Life and even, in another sense, The Birth of a Nation. There is the ethical problem of how Black character was portrayed by white directors and scriptwriters who themselves either believed in or were indifferent about the stereotypes and misconceptions they were perpetuating. There is the practical problem of how aspiring Black actors, directors, producers, etc. were to gain access to a field that was determinedly closed against them. And there is, for the authors of the books, articles, and other materials cited here, the problem of gleaning and amassing informa-

1

tion, then evaluating it in an effort to present valid critical
analyses to their readers.

The attitudes permeating most of the materials dealing with Blacks in American films are sociological reflections of the attitudes of and toward Blacks in other social
areas. Reactions and responses to Black experiences in
films in any given era paralleled the reactions and responses
to Black experiences in American society.

One factor remains constant throughout the history of
Black involvement in films in the United States: Black protest against their treatment, status, condition, and prospects
both in film and society in general. For films, protest took
several forms: there was protest through the written word
in journal and newspaper articles--most of it in Black pub-
lications; protest through boycott of particularly offensive
films such as The Birth of a Nation; and protest through
films made by Blacks for Blacks in an effort to counter the
degrading images presented in white films. The feature
films of the Lincoln Motion Picture Company, a pioneer
organization that existed from 1916 to 1923, are examples.

The beginning years of the twentieth century saw
early evidence of the Black's willingness to express anger
against the images presented by white filmmakers. In 1905,
the Niagara Movement, precursor of the NAACP, was
organized. Its leaders, among them W. E. B. DuBois,
exemplified a middle-class Black force that deplored racism
and denounced the accommodationist pronouncements of
Booker T. Washington. This group argued for the dignity of
Blacks by advocating voting rights and equality of citizenship
for Blacks. They founded the periodical, Crisis Magazine,
as the official organ through which they expressed their

aggressively intellectual views. In May, 1917, <u>Crisis</u> reprinted an angry letter from the Dayton, Ohio <u>Forum,</u> denouncing some Black Daytonians who had purportedly prevented a protest against the showing of <u>The Birth of a</u>
<u>Nation</u> in Dayton from being successful.

The 1920's saw the burgeoning of the Harlem Renaissance. A new social force of Blacks, migrating to the northern big cities from the South during World War I, achieved notable successes in writing and on stage. Sophisticated literary works were produced by writers like Langston Hughes, Countee Cullen, Richard Wright and Claude McKay, who eloquently affirmed the pride of Blackness.

The thirties, with the depression, and the forties, through World War II, saw a continuation of intellectual attacks against racism in all aspects of American life, including films. <u>Crisis</u> and <u>Opportunity</u>, organ of the Urban League, kept up the fight with articles protesting demeaning stereotypes, directly challenging Hollywood on its policies. "Uncle Tom in Hollywood" was presented in the November 1934 issue of <u>Crisis.</u> Sterling A. Brown's editorial in the August 1935 issue of <u>Opportunity</u> criticized the portrayals in the movie, <u>Imitation of Life.</u> In October of 1935 <u>Opportunity</u> printed the article, "Hollywood Presents Us: the Movies and Racial Attitudes."

The forties saw Hollywood being taken on in earnest. <u>Negro Digest</u> printed several articles on Hollywood's relationship with Blacks: "How Hollywood Can Better Race Relations" appeared in November of 1947; "How Hollywood Feels about Negroes" in August of 1947; "Hollywood's New Deal for Negroes" in June of 1946; and in April 1943, "Is Hollywood Fair to Negroes in Its Films?"

The 1950's ushered in a new era of exploration of the
social "problem" presented by the American Black.   White
actors and directors spoke out on questions of Hollywood's
relation to Blacks.   The worlds of the Black and white con-
fronted each other: "She Passed for White--in the Movies"
was Negro Digest's March 1950 article about Jeanne Crain;
"Hollywood Director Speaks Out (on race relations)" was
the subject of one of a January 1951 presentation in the
same magazine.

Black actors had comments to make about their experiences as actors.   Our World printed a July 1951 article
entitled "Cry the Beloved Country: Visiting Actors Taste
South Africa's Race Hate."   "The Breaking Point," in
August 1951, has the actor Juano Hernandez remarking that
the film marked the first time that a Black man and a white
man were equals in a film.   Periodicals such as Our World,
Ebony, and Sepia played up the popular aspects of Black involvement in Hollywood.   Individual Black actors and actresses were ballyhooed; every achievement of Blacks was
underscored as another indication that Black artists and
artisans could be successful in this field.   Articles appeared
about movies such as Pinky and Lost Boundaries, which
dealt with "interracial" themes wherein the heroes and
heroines were portrayed as "tragic mulatto" types.

The late fifties and early sixties saw the advent of
the civil rights era.   Integration into the white cultural
mainstream became a prominent goal of Blacks, and this
aspiration was mirrored in the aspirations of Black actors
in films.   The late sixties, however, with its password of
"Black Power!", also ushered in intraracial conflict: dissatisfaction, belligerence, integration versus independence.

Blacks demanded to become arbiters of their own destinies
in all areas of American society. Discontent with the Black
image presented by Hollywood, pessimism that Hollywood
would ever change its ways, were expressed in various
articles. Negro History Bulletin's October 1960 issue offered
the article, "Hollywood Phony on Negro Films, Writer
Charges." "Not by Protest Alone!" in Negro Digest for
April of 1968 asserted that Black writers must create
plausible roles for Black actors and not wait for white
writers to do it. "Needed: a Negro Film Movement" was
an earlier rallying cry in January 1966. Dissatisfaction was
still being expressed later that year, in May 1966, with the
article "Hollywood and the Negro: the Slow Pace of Change."

The intraracial conflict was manifested in the attitudes
of some actors. Whereas before it was accepted that Blacks
should emulate whites in all fields, now it was expected that
a Black man should be Black first and anything else second.
Confusion resulted. "The Negro Actor Asks Himself: Am
I a Negro or Am I an Actor?" appeared in the October 15,
1967 issue of the New York Times Magazine, while the
Hollywood Reporter of June 4, 1968 attributes to actor
Yaphet Kotto the statement that "Negro actors should act,
not be diverted."

The seventies brought the "Black boom" in movies.
Films such as Shaft and Superfly were box-office smashes,
seen by both whites and Blacks, but cashing in to a large
degree on the Black market. This prompted a spate of
analyses and reactions from the white press as well as the
Black. "Black Movies: Renaissance or Rip-off?" asks
Newsweek in its October 23, 1972 issue. "New Films: Culture or Con Game?" wonders Ebony in the issue of December, 1972.

The financial success of these movies, at a time when the motion picture industry seemed to be failing, stimulated a further rash of films, some produced by whites and some by Blacks. The first films of this "new" genre purported to portray the Black as he wished to be portrayed. It was the white man who always lost in these films, offering some cheer to Black audiences wearied by losing battles with the white culture in other areas.

It is perhaps still too early to evaluate fully the causes and effects of the "Black boom" in American films, but this bibliography attempts to offer useful guidance to the researcher who wishes to find the data to support an informed opinion on this and other aspects of the experiences of Blacks in American films.

NON-PERIODICAL REFERENCES

INDEXES

Black Information Index. Herndon, Virginia, Infonetics,
 Incorporated, Vol. 1, 1970. Bimonthly.
   (Published to disseminate information by and about
   Black people and their environment found in peri-
   odical materials.)

Index to Periodical Articles by and about Negroes, 1960-1970.
   Boston, G.K. Hall and Company, 1971.
   (Index to periodical materials in the Hallie Q. Brown
   Memorial Library at Central State University in Wil-
   berforce, Ohio and the Schomburg Collection of Negro
   Literature and History at the New York Public Li-
   brary.)

Index to Selected Periodicals, 1950-1959. Boston, G.K.
   Hall and Company, 1961.
   (Index to periodical materials in the Hallie Q.
   Brown Memorial Library at Central State University
   in Wilberforce, Ohio and the Schomburg Collection
   of Negro Literature and History at the New York
   Public Library.)

Reader's Guide to Periodical Literature. New York, H.W.
   Wilson Company, 1913- . Monthly.

Social Sciences and Humanities Index. New York, H.W.
   Wilson Company, 1907- . (Volumes 1-18 entitled
   International Index.)

7

BIBLIOGRAPHIES

Chicago Public Library, Chicago Afro-American Union Analy-
  tic Catalog. Boston, G. K. Hall and Company, 1972.
  (Five volumes. A "definitive bibliography of Afro-
  American literature in the United States from early
  times to 1940, using the resources ... found in the
  principal libraries of Chicago.")

Kirk, Sherri and Glenda Peace, Black Sojourn: A Bibli-
  ography. University of California, Davis, 1969.
  (Bibliography of selected materials from the U. C.
  Davis' African-Afro-American Collection.)
  See: "Literature, Drama, Music, Arts, Cookbooks."
  Sweet Flypaper of Life.

Miller, Elizabeth and Mary L. Fisher, The Negro in
  America: A Bibliography. Second edition, Cambridge,
  Massachusetts, Harvard University Press, 1970.
  ("Definitive documentation of [the] new and refresh-
  ing look at Negro Americans.")
  See: Chapter 7, "Theater, Dance and the Arts."

National Urban League, Selected Bibliography on the Negro.
  Fourth edition, New York, June, 1951.
  ("Compiled to assist those who wish to further ac-
  quaint themselves with the life and work of the Negro.")
  See: "Literature, Drama, Art, Music, Poetry."

Negro Bibliographic and Research Center, The Negro in
  Print. Bimonthly. Washington, May, 1965. Vol. 1.

New York Public Library, Black Films: A Selected List.
  New York, 1971.
  ("Lists films on Africa, civil rights and Black his-
  tory....")

New York Public Library, Dictionary Catalog of the Schomburg Collection of Negro Literature and History. Boston, G. K. Hall and Company, 1962.

New York Public Library, No Crystal Stair: A Bibliography
  of Black Literature, 1971.
  ("Lists significant books published since 1965."
  Also includes selected classic titles from earlier
  editions, which date from 1925.)

See Section: "Literature and the Arts: General
Works."

Porter, Dorothy B., comp. The Negro in the United States.
Washington, D.C., Library of Congress, 1970.
(Materials in the collections of the Library of Con-
gress and other libraries.)
See: "Entertainment."

Turner, Darwin T., comp. Afro-American Writers. New
York, Appleton-Century-Crofts, Educational Division,
1970.
("A convenient guide to drama, fiction, and poetry
by Afro-Americans and to scholarship about those
writers.")
See Sections: "Backgrounds": Art, Journalism,
Music, Theatre.

Welsh, Irwin K., The Negro in the United States: A Research Guide. Bloomington, Indiana University Press,
1965.
(Listing of and commentary on books, articles and
other materials that deal with Blacks from an historical perspective.)
See Chapter 4: "The Negro and the Arts."

GENERAL REFERENCE WORKS ON BLACKS

Davis, John P., The American Negro Reference Book.
Englewood Cliffs, N.J., 1966.
("A summary of current information on the main
aspects of Negro life in America.")
See Chapter 24: "The Negro and American Enter-
tainment," by Langston Hughes.

Ebony, The Negro Handbook, comp. by the editors of Ebony.
Chicago, Johnson Publishing Company, 1966.
("A [documentary of] the present-day status of the
Negro.")
See: 1. "The Negro in Hollywood"; 2. "Events in
Motion Pictures" (Awards, outstanding movies 1964-
1965).

Gumby, L. S. Alexander, Gumby Collection of American
     Negro Scrapbooks (circa 1890-1950).   Film, 17 reels.
     Reproduced from collection at Columbia University.
     Index or contents of collection at beginning of each
     reel.   Reels have scrapbook information on Green
     Pastures (reel 5), moving pictures (reel 8), Negro
     entertainers (reel 10), Paul Robeson (reel 14), etc.

Johnson, George P. , Negro Film Collection.   UCLA Oral
     History Department, Los Angeles, 1970.
        (Scrapbooks, articles, and other personal mementoes
        of George P. Johnson.   Special collections.)

The Negro Handbook, (Vols. 1-4).   New York, W. Malliet
     and Company, 1942-1949.   Florence Murray, editor,
     1942.
        (Collection of facts and figures concerning Blacks.)

Ploski, Harry A. , and Ernest Kaiser, The Negro Almananc.
     New York, The Bellwether Company, 1971.
        ("A comprehensive reference work ... on the his-
        tory and culture of black Americans and their signif-
        icant contributions to our society. ")
        See: Section 20, "The Black Entertainer in the Per-
        forming Arts. " Movies.

Work, Monroe Nathan, Negro Yearbook, An Annual Ency-
     clopedia of the Negro.   1912-1919, 1922, 1925-26,
     1931-38.
        ("An annual Encyclopedia of the Negro. ")

DISSERTATIONS

Bloom, Samuel W. , A Social Psychological Study of Motion
     Picture Audience Behavior: a Case Study of the Negro
     Image in Mass Communication.   University of Wiscon-
     sin, 1956.
        (An analysis of the contents and the effect of the
        movie Lost Boundaries.)

Goldberg, Albert L. , The Effects of Two Types of Sound
     Motion Pictures on Attitudes of Adults toward Minority
     Groups.   Indiana University, 1956.

EXCERPTS

Adler, Renata, A Year in the Dark; A Year in the Life of a
    Film Critic. Berkley Medallion Edition, New York, 1971.
        See: "The Negro that movies overlook: stereotypes. "

Beck, Marilyn, Marilyn Beck's Hollywood, New York, Haw-
    thorne Books, Inc. , 1973.
        See: "Hollywood discovers 'the Black Market'--and
        learns that Blacks, like whites, dig violence. "

Crist, Judith, The Private Eye, the Cowboy, and the Very
    Naked Girl: Movies from Cleo to Clyde. N. Y. , Holt, 1968.
        (Addresses, essays, and lectures.)

Cruse, Harold, The Crisis of the Negro Intellectual. New
    York, William Morrow and Company, Inc. , 1967.
        See: "Intellectuals and the Theater of the 1960s--as
        medium and dialogue. " See also: Index entries,
        "Film Industry, " "Movie Industry. "

Everson, William K. A Pictorial History of the Western
    Film. Secaucus, N. J. , Citadel Press, 1969.
        (Contains commentary on such "inept" productions of
        Black westerns as Bronze Buckaroo and Harlem
        Rides the Range.)

Geduld, Harry, editor, Focus on D. W. Griffith. Englewood
    Cliffs, N. J. , Prentice-Hall, 1971.
        (One of the Film Focus series. Contains articles
        and essays by and about David Wark Griffith includ-
        ing "How I Made Birth of a Nation. ")

Griffith, Richard, The Movie Stars. Garden City, New
    York, Doubleday and Company, 1970.
        (Contains a short commentary in Chapter III, Section
        8, entitled "Dislike me not for my complexion, "
        whose contention seems to be that Hollywood has ac-
        cepted Blacks and other dark-skinned minorities be-
        cause of pressure, not demand.)

Lawson, John H. , Film in the Battle of Ideas. New York,
    Masses and Mainstream, 1953.
        (Blacks in film from politico-economic viewpoint.)

Miller, Edwin, "Seventeen" Interviews: Film Stars and

Superstars. London, Macmillan Company; New York,
Collier-Macmillan Ltd. , 1970.
    (Seventeen magazine's collection of articles on vari-
    ous film stars, including a short chapter on Sidney
    Poitier.)

Newquist, Roy, A Special Kind of Magic. Chicago, Rand
    McNally, 1967.
    (With discussions by Sidney Poitier.)

Ross, Theodore T. , Film and the Liberal Arts. New York,
    Holt, Rinehart and Winston, 1970.
    (Contains material on Blacks in motion pictures:
    "Black men or good niggers?")

Shales, Tom, editor, The American Film Heritage. Wash-
    ington, D. C. , Acropolis Books, Ltd. , Publication of
    the American Film Institute, 1972.
    (Impressions from the American Film Institute
    Archives. Collection of writeups on American films,
    including ten pages on the history of Blacks in film
    from Spyin' the spy (1917) to Sweetback; and the
    article The Emperor Jones by Tom Shales.)

EXTRACTS

Cripps, Thomas R. ,   "Myth of the Southern Boxoffice: a
    Factor in Racial Stereotyping in American Movies,
    1920-1940, " in The Black Experience in America:
    Selected Essays, ed. by James Curtis and Lewis Gould.
    Austin, Texas, University of Texas Press, 1970.

Killens, John Oliver, "Hollywood in Black and White, " in
    White Racism; Its History, Pathology, and Practice,
    ed. by Barry Schwartz and Robert Disch. New York,
    Dell Publishing Co. , Laurel Editions, 1970.

Miller, Loren, "Uncle Tom in Hollywood, " in The Negro in
    American History: Black Americans 1928-1968, Vol. 1,
    eds. Mortimer J. Adler, Charles Van Doren and George
    Ducas. Encyclopaedia Britannica Educational Corp. , 1969.
    (Discussion of the perpetuation of Black stereotypes
    by Hollywood movies of the 30's. Originally in Crisis,

41:329₊.)

Zito, Stephen, "The Black Film Experience," in The American Film Heritage, ed. by Tom Shales. Washington,
D.C., Acropolis Books, Ltd., 1972.

BOOKS

Bogle, Donald, Toms, Coons, Mulattoes, Mammies and
Bucks: An Interpretative History of Blacks in American
Films. New York, Viking Press, 1973.
(The history of Blacks in American cinema is one
of stereotypes. All Black actors have played stereotyped roles, but the essence of Black film history
is not found in the stereotyped role but in what certain talented actors have done with the stereotypes,
from 1903 to the 70's.)

Bond, Frederick W., The Negro and the Drama; the Direct
and Indirect Contribution which the American Negro Has
Made to Drama and the Legitimate Stage. College
Park, Maryland, McGrath Publishing Company, 1969.
(The author's intention is "to determine the elements
which motivated and inspired the American Negro to
enter the field of drama as a profession....")
Of special interest: Chapter 10, "Negro Drama in
Moving Pictures and Radio."

Chambers, Lucille Arcola, ed., America's Tenth Man: A
Pictorical Review of One-Tenth of a Nation, Presenting
the Negro Contribution to American Life Today. New
York, Twayne Publishers, Inc., 1957.
See: "Motion Picture Digest."

Ellis, Shirley, The Negro in American Film. New York,
United States Information Service, 1957.

Fletcher, Tom, One Hundred Years of the Negro in Show
Business. New York, Burdge, 1954.

Hughes, Langston, and Milton Meltzer, Black Magic: A Pictorial History of the Negro in American Entertainment.
Englewood Cliffs, New Jersey, Prentice-Hall, 1967.

Isaacs, Edith J. , The Negro in the American Theatre. New
    York, Theatre Arts, 1947.

Jerome, Victor Jeremy, The Negro in Hollywood Films.
    New York, Masses and Mainstream, 1950.
        (A "Marxist indictment of American films of the 40's.
        dealing with racial themes. " The author believes
        that the stereotyped portrayals of Black characters
        would help perpetuate the American Black's condi-
        tion.)

Mapp, Edward, Blacks in American Films: Today and Yes-
    terday. Metuchen, New Jersey, Scarecrow Press,
    1972.
        (The objective of the book is to "ascertain by use of
        informal qualitative content analysis the portrayal of
        the Negro as a major character in recent American
        films. Emphasis is placed on an objective assess-
        ment of the content of the Negro portrayal. " Analy-
        sis of films of the 60's. Bibliography.)

Mitchell, Loften, Black Drama: The Story of the American
    Negro in the Theater. New York, Hawthorn, 1967.
        (The history of Black drama, especially in Harlem,
        from the 17th century to the 1960's. The author con-
        tends that "in America the theater has reflected the
        society which has stood on the Negro's shoulders,
        yet failed to acknowledge this. . . . ")

Noble, Peter, The Cinema and the Negro, 1905-1948. Lon-
    don, 1948.
        (Index to the work of Negro actors in the cinema:
        the most important productions of the previous fifty
        years containing parts for Negroes or touching on
        racial themes generally. American, British, and
        Continental--French, German, Russian--films. Listed
        by name of film in chronological order.)

Noble, Peter, The Negro in Films. London, S. Robinson,
    1948.
        (Traces the experience of the Negro from the earli-
        est silent films up to the motion pictures of post-
        World War II European films.

Null, Gary, Black Hollywood: The Negro in Motion Pictures.
    New York, Citadel Press, to be published in 1974.

Patterson, Lindsay,   Anthology of the American Negro in the
    Theater: A Critical Approach.   New York, Publishers
    Company, 1967.

Pines, Jim,   Blacks in the Cinema: The Changing Image.
    London, Education Department, British Film Institute,
    1971.
        (An historical assessment of stock-type figures in
        relation to cultural aspects of the Black community
        and American society.   Definition of the role mass
        cultural media have played in Black political and cul-
        tural affairs.   Contains a filmography of most im-
        portant films made about Blacks from 1950, plus
        others from the 20's, 30's, and 40's.)

Rollins, Charlemae Hill,   Famous Negro Entertainers of
    Stage, Screen, and Television.   New York, Dodd, Mead
    and Company, 1967.
        (Contains biographies of such stars as Harry Bela-
        fonte, Bert Williams, Lena Horne, Paul Robeson,
        Bill Robinson, Eartha Kitt.)

Sprecher, Daniel, ed.,   Guide to Films About Negroes.
    Alexandria, Virginia, Serina, 1970.

BIOGRAPHIES AND AUTOBIOGRAPHIES

Bailey, Pearl.
    The Raw Pearl.   New York, Harcourt, 1968.

Dandridge, Dorothy.
    Dandridge, Dorothy, and Earl Conrad,   Everything and
    Nothing: the Dorothy Dandridge Tragedy.   New York,
    Abelard, 1970.

Davis, Ossie.
    Funke, Lewis,   The Curtain Rises: the Story of Ossie
    Davis.   New York, Grosset, 1971.
        (For young people.)

Dee, Ruby.
    In: Fax, Elton C.,   Contemporary Black Leaders.
    New York, Dodd, 1970.

Poitier, Sidney.
    Hoffman, William, <u>Sidney</u>. Secaucus, N.J., Lyle
    Stuart, Inc., 1971.

    In: Gross, Theodore L., ed. <u>Representative Men.</u>
    New York, Free Press, 1970.

    In: Walker, Alexander, <u>Stardom</u>. Stein, 1970.

Waters, Ethel.
    <u>To Me It's Wonderful</u>. New York, Harper, 1972.

Toppin, Edgar A., <u>The Biographical History of Blacks in</u>
    <u>America Since 1528.</u> New York, McKay, 1971.
    (Based on a series of weekly articles in <u>The Christian</u>
    <u>Science Monitor</u>, March 6-June 12, 1969. Included:
    Harry Belafonte, Diahann Carroll, Sidney Poitier,
    Bert Williams, Ethel Waters, Bill Robinson, Paul
    Robeson.)

SUBJECT LISTING OF PERIODICAL CITATIONS

Summary of Contents

History of Blacks in Films	18
Blacks and Films	19
Blacks and Hollywood	23
Blacks and Whites	31
Black Films, Filmmakers, Filmmaking	33
The Black Image	38
Men	40
Women	41
The Black "Boom"	41
Comments and Criticism	42
Film and Black Athletes	45
Black Musicians and Music	47
Actors and Actresses	48
Movies	57
Blacks, Films, and Politics	66
Blacks, Films, and Social Tensions	67

THE LISTING

HISTORY OF BLACKS IN FILMS

1. "'Black America' focus on Hollywood influence," Film-TV Daily, June 25, 1968.

2. "Black American cinema: A primer," Norman Kagan, Cinema, 6:2, Fall, 1970.
    (A history of early Black filmmaking.)

3. "Blaxploitationers of 1972," Variety Weekly, Jan. 3, 1973.
    (Black image in film is concern of such groups as the Coalition Against Blaxploitation (CAB) and the Black Artists Alliance.)

4. "First Black movie stars;" excerpts from Toms, Coons, Mulattoes, Mammies and Bucks, D. Bogle, Saturday Review Arts, 1:25-9, Feb. 1973.

5. "Gamut from A to B: the image of the Black in pre-1915 movies," Political Science Quarterly, 88:53-70, March 1973.

6. "History of a dream: relating the birth and travails of the American Negro theatre," W. E. B. Dubois, New York Times, Sept. 24, 1944.

7. "Looking back on Blacks in films; excerpts from and comments on Donald Bogle's Toms, Coons, Mulattoes, Mammies and Bucks." Ebony, 28:35-44A.

8. "Movies in the ghetto B. P. (Before Poitier)," Negro Digest, 18:21-27, Fall 1969.

9. "Negro films," Sight and Sound, 18:27-30, Jan. 1950.
    (Discussion of Pinky, Home of the Brave, and Lost boundaries.)

18

10.   "Negro in the American theatre: a record of achieve-
      ment, " E. J. Isaacs, Theatre Arts, 26:492-543,
      August, 1942.

11.   "100 years of Negro entertainment, " Allan Morrison,
      Ebony, 18:122-4, Sept. 1963.

12.   "Rise of Negro matinee idol: new image of American
      Black, " Robert H. Welker. Variety Weekly, Feb.
      1961, p. 7.
            (Short history of Black movie stars, such as Bill
            Robinson, Canada Lee, Harry Belafonte.)

BLACKS AND FILMS

13.   "All-American newsreel, " Daily Variety, Mar. 7, 1945.

14.   "American in Italian movies, " Ebony, 15:85-86+,
      June, 1960.
            (Edith Peters.)

15.   "Ancient film's effect on modern Negro life, " Roy Wil-
      kins, Los Angeles Times, Feb. 15, 1965.
            (The Birth of a Nation)

16.   "Belafonte: 'Look, ' they tell me, 'don't rock the boat;
      play nice guy, play dead or maybe play a super-Negro
      who beats up communists', " Harry Belafonte, New
      York Times, Apr. 21, 1968.

17.   "Black cinema expo., '72; Black cinema library-re-
      search center, " Ebony, 27:151-4, May 1972.

18.   "Black film festival now offered in Indianapolis, " Box
      Office, May 14, 1973.

19.   "Black movies/Black theatre, " J. P. Murray, The
      Drama Review, 16:56-61, Dec. 1972.

20.   "Film as a tool for liberation?" Black Creation, 4:36-
      37, Winter 1973.

21.   "The film gains a dimension, " Quarterly of Film,
      Radio and Television, 7:77+, Fall, 1952.

22. "First African movie made by and about Africans made by Ossie Davis, " J. Bennett, Sepia, 20:59-63, Sept. 71.

23. "Guess who's coming to cinema?" Edward Mapp, Movie/TV Marketing, 24:44, Mar. 70.

24. 'Haiti goes to the movies; 20th Century stages junket to show off Lydia Bailey, " Our World, 7:46-53, Aug. 1952.

25. 'He who must die, " Liberation, 4:17-18, Mar. 1959.

26. 'Italy's film industry may top Hollywood in lifting bias as Negro roles soar, " Variety Weekly, June 12, 1968, p. 30.

27. "Jedda; colored Australians star in new movie, " Ebony, 12:108+, Mar. 1957.

28. "Lydia Bailey: Negro history glorified in superb new movie on Haiti during days of Toussaint, " Ebony, 7:39-44, Jan. 1952.

29. 'Mambo: Katherine Dunham has choice acting, dancing, singing role in new Italian music drama, " Ebony, 10: 83-84+, Dec. 1954.

30. "More Italo pic parts for U. S. Negroes, " Daily Variety, June 7, 1968.

31. "Needed: a Negro film movement, " Walter Moore, Negro Digest, 15:45-48, Jan. 1966.

32. "The Negro actor asks himself, 'Am I a Negro or am I an actor?'" New York Times Magazine, 34-5, Oct. 15, 1967.

33. "Negro actors in dramatic roles, " America, 115:298-300, Sept. 17, 1966.

34. "Negro actors win roles in German films and TV; Orphan (Elfie Fiegert) to star at 17, " Variety Weekly, July 31, 1963.

35. "The Negro in American films, " Carlton Moss, Freedomways, 3:135-142, Spring, 1963.

36.   "The Negro in American films: Some recent works, "
       Albert Johnson, Film Quarterly, 18:14-30, Summer
       1965.
            (Discussion of efforts to portray the Black "prob-
            lem" in several movies of the 60's.)

37.   "Negro in the American theater, " Negro Digest, 11:
       52-58, July 1962.

38.   "The Negro in cinema, " Earl Cameron, Films and
       Filming, 3:9-11, May 1957.
            ("The color bar in the studios is being broken. ")

39.   "The Negro in entertainment, " Quick News Weekly,
       Aug. 13, 1951.

40.   "The Negro in films: Old issue raised by new screen
       items, " Bosley Crowther, New York Times, Oct. 6,
       1963.

41.   "The Negro in films: Poitier points a dilemma which
       The Cool World helps rebut. " New York Times, Apr.
       26, 1964.

42.   "The Negro in films today, " Arthur Knight, Films in
       Review, Feb. 1950, pp. 14-19.

43.   "The Negro in show business, " Negro Digest, Paul
       Denis, 1:34, Feb. 1943.

44.   "Negro pioneers comment, " Variety Weekly, Dec. 27,
       1967.
            (Vincent Tubbs of the Publicists' Guild and A. S.
            "Doc" Young of the Los Angeles Sentinel offer
            corrective comments on article "One-third film
            public: Negro" in Nov. 29, 1967 issue of Weekly
            Variety.)

45.   "The Negro theatre, " Brown American, Dec. 1936.

46.   "Negroes and the box office, " Variety Weekly, Nov.
       29, 1967.
            (Negroes represent one-third of the ticket buyers
            in the U. S. film market.... This must ... but-
            tress the case for a more open-minded use of
            Negro actors in the production side of the indus-
            try....)

47.   "Negroes movie-conscious; support 430 film houses, "
      Motion Picture Herald, Jan. 24, 1942, pp. 33-34.

48.   "Not by protest alone!" Negro History Bulletin, 31:12-
      14, April 1968.
            (Young black playwrights must make the Black
            characters plausible so that Blacks may get roles
            in films and on stage.)

49.   "One-third film public: Negro, " Lee Beaupre. Vari-
      ety Weekly, Nov. 29, 1967. pp. 3, 61.
            ("Film companies are gradually learning that black
            power can also mean green power.... The racial
            prejudice evidenced by earlier Hollywood films cer-
            tainly affected Negro filmgoers, especially chil-
            dren.... the Negro is usually present as a noble
            primitive or a sepia-toned white man. ")

50.   "Passing years, " Negro History Bulletin,   22:93-4,
      Jan. 1959.

51.   "Pro-Negro films in Atlanta, " [reprint from Films in
      Review, Nov. 1952], Gerald Weales, Phylon, 13:298-
      304, Dec. 1952.
            (Analysis of reactions in Atlanta to such films as
            Pinky, Home of the Brave, Intruder in the Dust.)

52.   "Problems facing Negro actors, " Woodie King, Jr.,
      Negro Digest, 15:53-59, April 1966.

53.   "Sailor to movie star, " Ebony, 8:46-51, August 1953.
            (Japanese problem film makes star of Navy's
            Danny Williams.)

54.   "Sepia visits a filming, " A. S. Young, Sepia, 56-61.
      June 1960.

55.   "Star of Italian movies: John Kitzmiller picked for role
      while playing poker, " Ebony, 7:71-73, Nov. 1951.

56.   "Steel helmet: first movie about Korean War has excel-
      lent role of Negro medical corpsman, " Ebony, 6:78-
      80, Mar. 1951.

57.   "They made him a saint, " Sepia, 16:60-63, Oct. 1967.
            (Cuban actor, Rene Munoz.)

58.   "Tokyo's little mister star, "   M. Goodwin and A.
      Brown, Sepia, 9:38-40, Feb. 1961.
            (Clinton Mumford)

59.   "Within our gates, "   Chicago Defender, Jan. 10, 1920,
      p. 6.
            (Latest Micheaux production.)

BLACKS AND HOLLYWOOD

60.   "Actors and other minority groups, "   Charlton Heston,
      Journal of the Producer's Guild of America,   10:35-37,
      Mar. 1968.

61.   "Actors show how" [editorial], Negro Digest, 2:63-64,
      April 1944.
            (Absence of discrimination in the union, Actors
            Equity Association.)

62.   "After 'big' scare, Hollywood using darkest Negroes
      around, reports colored actress, "   Daily Variety, Oct.
      11, 1963.
            (Mittie Lawrence, on fair employment investiga-
            tions.)

63.   "An assessment of the status of Hollywood Blacks, "
      Dan Knapp, Los Angeles Times Calendar.   Sept. 28,
      1969.
            (Probing progress of minorities in Los Angeles
            segments of film, radio, television, and recording
            industries.)

64.   "Black Capitalism big factor in PUSH drive in Holly-
      wood, "   Will Tusher, The Hollywood Reporter, Aug. 18,
      1972.

65.   "Brock Peters on Negro skepticism: one colored star
      hardly a trend, "   Lee Beaupre, Variety Weekly, Dec.
      20, 1967.
            ("Sidney Poitier's ascension to superstar status ...
            has not opened many doors for other Negro per-
            formers. ")

66.   "Burt Lancaster sees Negro advance in films, "   Film

Daily, Mar. 1, 1968.

67.   "Businessmen push fair job drive; movie urging decent
       jobs for Negroes produced by Illinois Chamber of Com-
       merce, " Ebony, 6:15-18+.   August, 1951.

68.   "Carmen Jones' boxoffice click improves Negro casting
       chances; may do O'Neill's 'Emperor Jones', " Variety
       Weekly, Feb. 23, 1955.

69.   "Central hires Negro, " Hollywood Reporter, July 13,
       1967.
              (Central Casting Corporation, for the first time in
              its history, hired a Negro, Floyd Holly, as a
              casting director trainee.   Holly had been an extra
              in Hollywood for the last three years.)

70.   "Color bar dissolves on selling, Negro actors find, "
       Bob Hull, Hollywood Reporter, May 6, 1968.
              (Cynical as the statement may appear, the only
              way Negroes will get ahead in show business is by
              demonstrating they are commercially acceptable.)

71.   "Columbia's Negro biz pitch: full drive for 10 pix in
       1965, " Variety Weekly, Jan. 13, 1967, p. 7.

72.   "Columbia Pictures names Negro as a corporate offi-
       cer, " Variety Weekly, Aug. 20, 1969.
              (George Marshall named assistant secretary of
              Columbia Pictures.)

73.   "The day Black movie stars got militant, " Black Cre-
       ation, 4:40, Winter 1973.
              (Formation of the Black Artists Alliance for quality
              presentation and representation of Blacks in films.)

74.   "'Definite increase' in Hollywood jobs for Negro per-
       formers reported by largest colored talent agency, "
       Daily Variety, Aug. 21, 1963.

75.   "Do Black actors make good fathers?" Sepia, 18:32-
       34, Dec. 69.

76.   "Do Negroes have a future in Hollywood?" Ebony, 11:
       24, Dec. 1955.

77.   "Film executive blames hiring bias on unions, " Robert

Kistler, <u>Los Angeles Times</u>, Oct. 19, 1969.
(Cause of discrimination linked to long-standing
union seniority rules.)

78.   "Goal: a Negro in every crew; pressures if IATSE re-
      sists. " Michael Fessier, Jr. , <u>Variety Weekly</u>, July
      24, 1963.

79.   "Goldwyn, Jr. , Negro feature series to star Raymond
      St. Jacques, Godfrey Cambridge, and Calvin Lockhart, "
      <u>Daily Variety</u>, April 3, 1969.

80.   "A Hollywood actress looks at the Negro, " Marsha
      Hunt, <u>Negro Digest</u>, 5:14-17, Sept. 1947.

81.   "Hollywood acts on race problem: employment of Negro
      actors shows marked rise, " <u>New York Times,</u> Sept.
      21, 1963, p. 82.

82.   "Hollywood and the Black man, " Paul Ringe, <u>Show</u>,
      September 1972, p. 61.

83.   "Hollywood and the Negro: the slow pace of change, "
      Robert G. Hunter, <u>Negro Digest</u>, 15:37-41, May 1966.

84.   "Hollywood change: Negroes gain in a new movie [<u>Kisses</u>
      <u>for my President</u>] and elsewhere, " Larry Green, <u>New</u>
      <u>York Times,</u> Sept. 22, 1963.

85.   "Hollywood director speaks out, " Robert Ellis, <u>Negro</u>
      <u>Digest,</u> 9:42-44, Jan. 1951.
             (Director Mark Robson talks about race in movies.)

86.   "Hollywood gives more work, roles to Negro: industry
      program also seeks to end 'servant' stereotype in film
      parts, " Harry Bernstein, <u>Los Angeles Times,</u> March
      13, 1966, p. A2.

87.   "Hollywood lauded on Negro hiring: spectacular improve-
      ment, " <u>Hollywood Citizen-News,</u> Dec. 2, 1964.

88.   "Hollywood NAACP in stepped-up pitch for Negro film-
      TV production employment, " <u>Variety Weekly,</u> July 28,
      1965.

89.   "Hollywood phony on Negro films, " <u>Negro History Bul-</u>
      <u>letin,</u> p. 21, Oct. 1960.

90.   "Hollywood report: unchanging attitude of whites towards
      the Negro, " Phylon, 6:13-16, Winter 1945.

91.   "Hollywood stunt girl, " Walter Burrell, Ebony, 27:147-
      148+, Dec. 1971.
      (Peaches Jones)

92.   "Hollywood's new breed, " Sepia, 12:20-25, June 1963.

93.   "Hollywood's new deal for Negroes, " John T. McManus
      and Louis Kronenberger, Negro Digest, 6:77-80, June
      1946.

94.   "How Hollywood can better race relations, " John Gar-
      field, Negro Digest, 6:4-8, Nov. 1947.

95.   "How Hollywood feels about Negroes, " Robert Jones,
      Negro Digest, 5:4-8, Aug. 1947.

96.   "How Hollywood is smashing the colour bar, " Sidney
      Harmon, Films and Filming, 5:7+, March 1959.
      (The author contends that "films are now breaking
      the chains of racial prejudice, " citing Anna Lucasta
      and other films as examples.)

97.   "IATSE: no Negro need apply: locals stick to exclusion,"
      Variety Weekly, July 31, 1963, p. 7.
      (Opposition of International Alliance of Theatrical
      Stage Employes to NAACP's demands that Negroes
      be allowed to join unions.)

98.   "Ida Lupino brings new hope to Hollywood, " Robert
      Ellis, Negro Digest, 8:47-49, Aug. 1950.

99.   "Is Hollywood fair to Negroes in its films?" Negro
      Digest, 1:15-21, April 1943.

100. "It's another part of the jungle: COMPO fears its 'civil
      rights' confused with rights for Negroes, " Variety
      Weekly, Aug. 7, 1963.
      (COMPO--Council of Motion Picture Organizations.)

101. "Knock on any door: how single courtroom scene involv-
      ing Negro was screened in Humphrey Bogart's powder-
      puff version of Motley novel, " Ebony, 4:34-38, Jan.
      1949.

102. "Living Between Two Worlds, " Sepia, 13:62-66, Feb. 1964.

103. "Miss Dunham trains dancers for new film, " Ebony, 13:121-122, Oct. 1958.
      (Katherine Dunham does choreography for movie Green mansions.)

104. "Movie boycott threat, " Hollywood Citizen-News, Octtober 9, 1969.
      (Boycott threat unless Black actors allowed integral parts in films.)

105. "Movie star who hates his job, " Robert Ellis, Negro Digest, 9:81-83, Dec. 1950.
      ("Richard Widmark, who portrays hate-Negroes character in movie No way out, hates himself for playing such a part and says never, never again. ")

106. "Movies turn deaf ear to colored plea, " Christian Century, 47:1140, Sept. 24, 1930.
      (Editorial on the unheeding of Black protest against Birth of a Nation.)

107. "NAACP to mount drive in June for more jobs in pix, " Daily Variety, May 5, 1965.

108. "NCI director says report lied, only 1 Black trainee hired, " Jim Newsom, Hollywood Citizen-News, Oct. 14, 1969.

109. "NCOMP charges Hollywood lacks Black sensitivity, " Christian Century, 86:1157, Sept. 10, 1969.

110. "Negro actors in Hollywood clover, " Variety Weekly, June 3, 1964.
      (Result of the NAACP's drive on Hollywood nearly a year later.)

111. "Negro actors organization disputes Wilkins view of Hollywood, " Daily Variety, Dec. 9, 1964.
      (Denial that Negro employment gains in Hollywood were "spectacular. ")

112. "Negro critics form group, " Hollywood Citizen-News, Nov. 19, 1949.
      (Leading Negro critics and newspapermen, spurred

by three current Hollywood films about Negroes in
American life [including Home of the Brave], have
formed a Negro Critics Circle.)

113.   "Negro employment increases in films, " Gene Handsaker, Los Angeles Times, Sept. 11, 1967.
(Statistics kept by Davis Roberts, Black actor and
an official of the Beverly Hills-Hollywood Branch of
the NAACP. Comments on the "new Negro stereotype": the well-groomed man with briefcase and no
real involvement in the plot.)

114.   "Negro film roles show sharp increase, " Hollywood
Citizen-News, Apr. 22, 1969.
(Negro roles in motion pictures are four times
greater today than they were three years ago.)

115.   "Negro lobby in Hollywood, " David O. Selznick,
Negro Digest, 4:27-28, Aug. 1946.

116.   "Negroes included as trainees at Metro and Revue-
Universal; stress on qualification for tasks, " Variety
Weekly, July 17, 1963.

117.   "Negroes still given racially oriented pic roles: O.
Davis, " Allen C. Lobsenz, Film Daily, Oct. 1, 1965.

118.   "Negroes 'written out' of Hollywood movies, " Los
Angeles Sentinel, May 9, 1946.
(Article on Leon H. Hardwick's article, "Screen
Stereo-types, " in May, 1946 issue of Negro Digest.)

119.   "No color line in casting: (Jim) Brown and Raquel
Welch, " Film-TV Daily, May 24, 1968.

120.   "Non-acting film, video jobs for Blacks up 48% in
1969, " Vance King, Film-TV Daily, March 12, 1970.

121.   "The Peanutman: new film indicts Hollywood race
bias, " Ebony, 2:48-50, July 1947.
(45-minute featurette about Dr. George Washington
Carver.)

122.   "Peck on prejudice, " Negro Digest, Anne Strick, 4:
27-28, Aug. 1946.

123.   "PUSH study shows systematic blackout of Blacks con-

tinues, " Hollywood Reporter, Nov. 8, 1972, p. 11.

124.   "Race talks in Hollywood, " Motion Picture Herald,
       Aug. 7, 1963.
              (On the fair employment practices' series of talks
              in Hollywood.)

125.   "Race tolerance: newest box office hit, " Peggy Weil,
       Negro Digest, 6:46-49, Aug. 1948.

126.   "Real anger was backstage; racial tensions during
       shooting of Halls of Anger, " Life, 69:50-2, August 21,
       1970.

127.   "Rights drive spurs casting of Negroes in movies,
       television shows: They get 41 roles in Warner's film
       [Kisses for my President]; NAACP seeks bigger parts,
       theaters boycott, " Wall Street Journal, Sept. 24, 1963.

128.   "Secret of a movie maid, " Ebony, 5:52-56+, Nov.
       1949.
              (Lillian Moseley)

129.   "A Star Is Born, " Ebony, 10:90-94 Jan. 1955.
              (New movie gives talented pair of youngsters chance
              to film big time: Patricia Rosamond and Bobby
              Sailes.)

130.   "Stardom 'for Negroes only', " Don Deleihbur, Negro
       Digest, 3:87-88, Nov. 1944.
              (Discrimination against mulattoes in show business.)

131.   "Thesps from racial minorities getting 8-9% of roles
       in Hollywood pix and TV, " A. D. Murphy, Daily Vari-
       ety, March 14, 1966.

132.   "They live on the edge of Hollywood, " A. S. Young,
       Sepia, 10:29-32, Nov. 1961.
              (Blacks in Hollywood.)

133.   "They made good in the movie capital, " William
       Smallwood, Opportunity, 19:76-77, Mar. 1941.
              (Hazel Washington and Mildred Blount, leather-
              worker and hatmaker for movie stars.)

134.   "This may be year industry makes itself clear as far
       as Negro is concerned, says Brock Peters, " Holly-

wood Reporter, Feb. 12, 1968.

135.   "Token use of Negroes in pix and television could be
       dangerous, " Dave Kaufman, Daily Variety, Jan. 23,
       1969.

136.   "Tony Curtis photographs Sergeants Three, " Ebony,
       17:43-44+, Apr. 1962.

137.   "[Vincent] Tubbs first Negro film council rep. , " Daily
       Variety, July 5, 1963.

138.   "U. S. Equal Employment Opportunity Commission calls
       for job bias suit against giant movie makers, " Jet,
       35:58-59, April 3, 1969.

139.   "U. S. plans to prod film industry on job discrimination
       charge, " Vincent T. Burke, The Los Angeles Times,
       Oct. 19, 1969.
          (Justice Department reportedly has evidence to war-
          rant suits against six movie studios and two T. V.
          networks.)

140.   "Valenti lauds Hyman for hiring Negro director, " Daily
       Variety, May 13, 1968.
          (On the hiring of Gordon Parks by Warner Bros. -
          Seven Arts.)

141.   "Wanted: Black talent: apply Hollywood, " Sepia, 17:
       16-18, Oct. 1968.

142.   "What makes Ron Rich run?" Sepia, 15:44-48, July,
       1966.

143.   "Why I played a film bigot, " Bobby Darin, Ebony, 18:
       45-46+, Nov. 1962.

144.   "Without Pity: Italian film stars John Kitzmiller in
       Negro-white love story, " Our World, 5:37, May 1950.

145.   "Writer says Blacks need own film heroes, " Hollywood
       Citizen-News, May 15, 1970.
          (Joe Greene, creator of Black fiction hero, "Super-
          spade. ")

146.   "[Darryl] Zanuck pledges fair 20th shake in casting Ne-
       groes, " Daily Variety, Oct. 4, 1962.

BLACKS AND WHITES

147. "Anna's sin: Italian film about interracial romance is
      first to allow Negro lover to win girl," Ebony, 9:33-
      36, Mar. 1953.

148   "Black Gold: routine horse-racing movie turns into
      challenging Hollywood document on racial tolerance,"
      Ebony, 2:39- Oct. 1947.

149. "The breaking point," Juano Hernandez, Our World,
      Aug. 1950.
          (Comment on the fact that this movie portrays a
          white man and a Black man as equals for the first
          time.)

150. "Cry the Beloved Country: novel makes moving, power-
      ful film on African race problem," Ebony, 6:57-62,
      July, 1951.

151. "Cry the Beloved Country: visiting actors taste South
      Africa's race hate while making movie," Our World,
      6:34-36, July 1951.

152. "The Defiant Ones: critics heap praise on bold movie,"
      Ebony, 13:80, Oct. 1958.

153. "Educational programs for the improvement of race
      relations: motion pictures, radio, the press and li-
      braries," Journal of Negro Education, 13:367-89, 1944.

154. "Guess who's coming to lunch?" Philip T. Hartung,
      Commonweal, 88:59, Aug. 23, 1968.

155. "He passed as a Negro," Al Weisman, Negro Digest,
      9:16-20, Oct. 1951.
          (Hollywood star Mel Ferrer is often mistaken for
          a Negro as a result of his role ... in ... Lost
          Boundaries.)

156. "Home of the Brave; Hollywood independent makes first
      film on anti-Negro bias." Ebony, 4:59-62, June 1949.

157. "I didn't want to play a bigot," Robert Ryan, Ebony,
      15:68-70+, Nov. 1959.

158.   "Island in the sun: Dandridge, Belafonte star in ro-
       mantic interracial film, " Ebony, 12:32-34+, July 1957.

159.   "Lights Out: story of blind GI's blasts racial bias in
       new movie, " Ebony, 6:87-88+, Dec. 1950.

160.   "Lost Boundaries: new film tells story of New England
       family that 'passed', " Ebony, 4:51-53, July 1949.

161.   "Mexico's interracial movie: film about blonde colored
       girl who has dark Negro baby is Latin American box
       office hit, " Ebony, 5:48-50, Feb. 1950.
          (Angelitos Negros.)

162.   "Mulatto; story of how an Italian came to accept his
       foster son born to his wife of an American Negro
       soldier, " Crisis, 57:698-699, Dec. 1950.

163.   "Negro and white love scenes that shock-it-to-you!"
       Coronet, April 1969, pp. 10-17.
          (On the breaking of the racial taboos in Hollywood
          films.)

164.   "No Way Out: story of Negro doctor is strongest of
       race-theme movies, " Ebony, 5:31-34, Mar. 1950.

165.   "Pinky: story of girl who passes will be most debated
       film of year, " Ebony, 4:23-25, Sept. 1949.

166.   "Pool of London: new British film tackles interracial
       romance with sensitivity and good taste not found in
       U. S. movies, " Ebony, 6:59-61, Oct. 1951.

167.   "President's lady; Vera Francis gets explosive role in
       movie touching on mixed romance theme, " Ebony, 8:
       71-75, Feb. 1953.

168.   "The problem, " Hollis Alpert, Saturday Review, 50:50,
       Jan, 21, 1967.
          (In "racial films such as Cool World and Nothing
          But a Man, etc., the "problem" seems to be that
          some people are white and others Black--and there's
          no way out of it.)

169.   "Sapphire: British film combines murder with inter-
       racial love, " Ebony, 15:51-54+, Dec. 1959.

170.   "She passed for Negro in the movies," Negro Digest,
       8:26-27, Mar. 1950.
       (Jeanne Crain.)

171.   "Senza pieta [Without Pity]: new Italian film handles
       touchy interracial theme," Ebony, 4:62-65, Nov. 1948.
       (With Black actor John Kitzmiller.)

172.   "Simba: powerful movie gives new view of violent Mau
       Mau conflict in East Africa," Ebony, 11:73-76, Jan.
       1956.

173.   "Two social scientists view No Way Out: the conscious
       versus the 'message' in an anti-bias film," Commen-
       tary, Martha Wolfenstein and Nathan Leites, 10:388-
       391, Oct. 1950.
       (Demonstrates "some of the ... complexities that
       face the producers of films intended to reshape
       racist attitudes.")

BLACK FILMS, FILMMAKERS, FILMMAKING

174.   "About Negro directors," Movie Mailbag, New York
       Times, December 24, 1967.
              (Letter written in refutation of a statement attrib-
              uted to Melvin Van Peebles to the effect that the
              Hollywood Screen Directors Guild kept Negroes out.
              Signed John Rich, Vice President, Directors Guild
              of America, Inc., Hollywood, California.)

175.   "Award goes to Negro for movie work," Los Angeles
       Times, Apr. 19, 1965.
              (Wendell Franklin, assistant director for The
              Greatest Story Every Told.)

176.   "Black backers set hard line: big demand for film
       dollar," Hollywood Reporter, Nov. 7, 1973, p. 3.
              (Money from the Black community going into film
              production is usually accompanied by a very tough
              attitude because Black financiers want to make
              money and they expect a lot of return for their
              investment.)

177.   "Black producers mass to generate financing," Will

Tusher, Hollywood Reporter, June 29, 1973, p. 1.

178.   "Brown outlines Black union plans 'self-determina-
       tion', " Collette Wood, Hollywood Reporter, Aug. 26,
       1969.
       (Jim Brown).

179.   "Chicago slums are recreated in Buenos Aires for
       film scene: Wright explains ideas about moving mak-
       ing, " Ebony, 6:84-85, Jan. 1951.
       (Native Son.)

180.   "A concerned filmmaker, " Business Screen, Sept. 1970.

181.   "The Cry of Jazz": Negro produced and directed doc-
       mentary film depicting through jazz the Negro's strug-
       gle ..., " Jet, p. 62, Feb. 18, 1960.

182.   "Director Ossie Davis talks about Black Girl, " Black
       Creation, 4:38-38, Winter 1973.

183.   "Distributor lists Negro pictures, " Motion Picture
       Herald, Aug. 15, 1968.

184.   "Don Williams: street kid to legitimate financial suc-
       cess, " Mary Murphy, Los Angeles Times, Mar. 24,
       1973.

185.   "5 Negro films to be made by Negroes, " Film Daily,
       Oct. 3, 1966.

186.   "Goldberg plans 12 Negro features, " Motion Picture
       Herald, Apr. 14, 1945.
       (Hollywood Pictures Corporation will produce 12
       feature films for the 1945-46 season; announced by
       Jack and Bert Goldberg.)

187.   "Gordon Parks" (interview), Essence, 3:62+, Oct. 1972.

188.   "Gordon Parks: The Learning Tree, " Sepia, 19:50-
       52+, April 1970.

189.   "Gordon Parks tells of union aid on Learning, " The
       Hollywood Reporter, Aug. 14, 1969.

190.   "Harry Belafonte's debut as a Hollywood producer, "
       Sepia, 7:34-39, July 1959.

191. "Hollywood hires a Negro director," Sepia, 12:35-38, Apr. 1963.
      (Wendell Franklin).

192. "Hollywood in the Bronx," Time, 5:35; 67, Jan. 29, 1940.
      (Micheaux Picture Corporation).

193. "The Independents: hard road for the old and new," Black Creation, 3:8-11, Spring 1972.

194. "How movies are made," Ebony, 2:40-43, Mar. 1947.
      ("How director William Crouch manages to turn out films for the Negro market on a mass production basis." Astor Pictures Company's Ebony Parade is featured.)

195. "Ike Jones' Embassy deal makes him first Negro to produce major pic," Variety Weekly, Sept. 1, 1965.

196. "Jesse Jackson applauds Save the Children as breakthrough film for Black moviemakers," Los Angeles Sentinel, Oct. 25, 1973, p. B9.

197. "Jewish museum's retrospective on Black filmmaking, back to 1916," Variety Weekly, Mar. 25, 1970.
      (Retrospective devoted to the works of various independent Black production companies such as the Lincoln Motion Picture Company and the Micheaux Film Company.)

198. "King, from Montgomery to Memphis," Ebony, 25: 172-174, April 1970.

199. "Makers of Black films stand at crossroads," L. A. Times Calendar, Jan. 28, 1973, p. 18.

200. "[Black films]: Many of 50 planned may not materialize, but 20 actually being developed," Daily Variety, Aug. 14, 1972.
      (Recent survey of Black-oriented releases, project developments and announcements yields the number 50, of which more than 20 are being developed.)

201. "Movie maker Belafonte," Ebony, 14:94-96, July 1959.

202. "Negro and Yiddish film boom," Herb Golden, Variety

Weekly, Jan. 3, 1940, p. 36.

203. "Negro 2d. assistant cameraman on London film [The
      Pawnbroker] speaks his mind: sees ad client, investor
      as 'foe,'" Variety Weekly, Oct. 13, 1963.

204. "Negroes into pix production; form inter-race casting
      plan," Dale Olson, Variety Weekly, May 19, 1965.

205. "New ideas urged for Negro movies," Los Angeles
      Sentinel, Apr. 4, 1946, p. 11.
          ("If Negro films are to survive and attract larger
          audiences, new ideas will have to replace the often
          repeated stereotyped subjects now used." Bill
          Alexander, President of Association of Negro Mo-
          tion Picture Producers in New York.)

206. "New producing unit for Negro talent," Hollywood Re-
      porter, Oct. 3, 1955.
          (The Splendora Film Corporation.)

207. "Peters forms Black production company, sets initial
      projects," Hollywood Reporter, Mar. 20, 1973.
          (Thomas A. Peters, founder of Indepth Productions,
          the "first Black filmmaking company offering com-
          plete services" in all types of films.)

208. "Power to the Peebles," Time, 98:47, Aug. 16, 1971.
          (Melvin Van Peebles)

209. "Primitive emotions aflame in a Negro film," Literary
      Digest, 103:42-56, Oct. 5, 1929.
          (Concerning a "talkie" dealing with the emotional
          aspects of Southern Negroes.)

210. "Producers suggest Negro job center," Hollywood Re-
      porter, Apr. 21, 1967.
          (Organizations interested in obtaining more employ-
          ment for Negroes in the motion picture and telefilm
          industry were asked by production companies,
          through the Association of Motion Picture and Tele-
          vision Producers, to set up a clearing house
          through which information about job openings can
          be distributed to members of the minority races.)

211. "Producers to make dignified pictures," Los Angeles
      Sentinel, May 9, 1946, p. 8.

(New York: Bill Alexander declared his company in
their [would-be] production of a full-length feature
presenting Negroes in an intelligent and dignified
manner, thus setting the pace for Hollywood to
follow. Associated Producers of Negro Motion Pictures, 121 E. 49th Street, New York. His first
four film shorts ready for distribution include The
Call of Duty, based on exploits of the Negro in the
Army, and The Highest Tradition, a Navy film on
the same order.)

212.   "Public finally to see documentary on Angela Davis,"
       Jet, 41:47, Nov. 25, 1971.

213.   "St. Clair Bourne: alternative Black visions," Michael
       Mattox, Black Creation, 4:32-34, Summer 1973.
       (Chamba Productions, Inc.)

214.   "The silent minority," Stephen Zito, American Film
       Report, May 1971, pp. 2-3.
       (Black film companies that made movies for Black
       audiences, such as the Lincoln Motion Picture
       Company, Micheaux Film Corporation, the Colored
       Players Film Corporation.)

215.   "Smith first Negro dialog coach," Daily Variety,
       Apr. 9, 1968.
       (Leonard Smith, hired by producer William Castle,
       is the first Negro to become a dialog coach on a
       major film, Paramount's The Riot.)

216.   "The Story of a Three-Day Pass: French film pushes
       Melvin Van Peebles into ranks of award-winning direc-
       tors," Ebony, 23:54-60, Sept. 1968.

217.   "Strange love story: Negro movie company with ...
       story on color prejudice among Negroes themselves,"
       Our World, 9:26-28, Mar. 1954.

218.   "Studio films schedules 12 Negro featurettes," Holly-
       wood Reporter, Jan. 12, 1955.

219.   "The subject is money," Black Creation, 4:26, Win.
       '73.

220.   "Sue Schapiro, lady movie producer," Sepia, 19:32-
       36, Aug. 1970.

221. "Texan to produce Negro pictures, " Los Angeles Sen-
     tinel, Apr. 25, 1946, p. 12.
          (Dallas: True Thompson to devote his time to the
          production of all-Negro motion pictures in conjunc-
          tion with Jack and Bert Goldberg of New York.
          Bert Goldberg has already produced Beale Street
          Mama. First production to be Dirty Gertie from
          Harlem USA.)

222. "232 Negro theatres 1-1/2% of all houses, " Motion
     Picture Herald, Apr. 24, 1937.

223. "Van Peebles on the inside, " Essence, 4:36+, Jun.
     1973.

224. "Which way the Black film?" Encore, 2:52-54, Jan.
     1973.

225. "Whitney Young urges Blacks set up their own production
     companies, " Daily Variety, Nov. 6, 1970.

226. "William Greaves: Creatively independent, " Black Cre-
     ation, 4:10-11, Fall 1972.

THE BLACK IMAGE

227. "Another kind of Negro stereotype, " Hal Humphrey.
     Los Angeles Times, Apr. 13, 1967, pt. 5, p. 20.
          (Television is ahead of the movies when it comes
          to integration and treating the Negro as a human
          being, Bill Cosby believes, but he continues to find
          plenty of indecision over "how to handle the
          Negro. ")

228. "Black imagery on the silver screen, " Essence, 3:34,
     Dec. 1972.

229. "Black screen image: where is it going in the seven-
     ties?" Walter Burrell, Soul Illustrated, Feb. 1970,
     pp. 19-20.

230. "Black vise tightens: demands censorship on Black pic-
     tures, " Will Tusher, Hollywood Reporter, Sept. 20,
     1972.

231. "Blackface, Hollywood style," Dalton Trumbo, Negro Digest, 2:37-39, Feb. 1944.

232. "Death of Rastus: Negroes in American films since 1945," Phylon, 28:267-275, Fall 1967.

233. "Era of dummies and darkies," Stephen Fay, Commonweal, 93:125-8, Oct. 30, 1970.

234. "Films, Poitier, and race riots," Robert J. Landry, Variety Weekly, Jan. 3, 1968, p. 12.
     (At this present point in U.S. history, U.S. film producers are ducking two great challenging themes, the war in Vietnam and the war in the Black urban ghetto.)

235. "Hollywood presents us," Cecil D. Halliburton, Opportunity, 13:296, Oct. 1935.

236. "Hollywood's Negroes mired in stereotypes," Burt Prelutsky, Los Angeles Times Calendar, Feb. 19, 1967, p. 9.
     (Stepin Fetchit ... and Sidney Poitier, two Negro film stars of different eras, are both victims of Hollywood penchant for stereotyping their race.)

237. "The honest movies about Negroes--when?" Renata Adler, Los Angeles Herald Examiner, Mar. 3, 1968.

238. "The image makers: Negro stereotypes," Negro History Bulletin, 26:127-28, Dec. 1962.

239. "Is Hollywood fair to Negroes in its films?" Negro Digest, 1:15-21, Apr. 1943.
     (Negro Digest poll.)

240. "Is it better to be Shaft than Uncle Tom?" New York Times, Aug. 26, 1973, p. D11.

241. "Old stereotyped pattern," George Yamada, Crisis, 60:17-19, Jan. 1953.

242. "Paul Robeson and Black identity in American movies," Massachusetts Review, 11:468-85, Summer 1970.

243. "The problem of Negro character and dramatic incident," William Couch, Jr., Phylon, 11:127-133, June 1950.

244.   "Re-evaluation needed in film industry," Charles
        Champlin, Los Angeles Times, Apr. 9, 1968, pt. 4,
        p. 1.
              (Hollywood's record regarding the Negro could be
              summed up by much the same phrase as covers the
              nation as a whole: some progress, not enough. Re-
              evaluation needed in the wake of Martin Luther
              King's assassination.)

245.   "A report on filmland," in column, "People and
        Places," Walter White, Chicago Defender, May 8, 1943.
              (Hollywood begins to deliver on its promises to
              broaden the treatment of Negroes in films.)

246.   "Screen stereotypes," Leon H. Hardwick, Negro Di-
        gest, 4:57-58, May 1946.

247.   "Stereotyping of Negroes in film," Vision, 1:69, '62.

248.   "The still invisible man," Peter Bart, New York
        Times, July 17, 1966.

249.   "Take two of a movie miracle," Art Seidenbaum, Los
        Angeles Times, Jan. 6, 1968, pt. B, p. 1.

250.   "Theatrical, TV film industries pledge to depict Ne-
        groes 'as in real life'," Daily Variety, Oct. 28, 1957.

251.   "To make the Negro a living human being," Lindsay
        Patterson, New York Times, Feb. 18, 1968, p. 8D.
              ("It has taken the Negro 100-odd show business
              years to live down the ... darky image ... only
              now to be saddled with another, that of the protest
              figure which seems to be ... as damaging and re-
              stricting for the Negro performer as the old ...
              one.")

252.   "Uncle Tom in Hollywood," Loren Miller, Crisis,
        41:329, Nov. 1934.
              (Protest against such films as Birth of a Nation.)

BLACK IMAGE: MEN

253.   "The Black man as movie hero: new films offer a
        different male image," Theophilus Green, Ebony, 27:
        144-148, Aug. 1972.

254. "Superspade's revenge, " National Review, 24:530-40,
      May 12, 1972.

BLACK IMAGE: WOMEN

255. "Ain't Beulah dead yet? or images of the Black woman
      in film, " Essence, 4:61₊, May, 1973.

256. "A bad Black image in film, " Essence, 4:70, May
      1973.

257. "Battle among the beauties: Black actresses vie for
      top movie roles, " Luci Horton, Ebony, 29:144-45 Nov.
      1973.
            (Pam Grier, Vonetta McGee, Gloria Hendry, Tamara
            Dobson.)

258. "The Black woman as a sex image in films, " Walter
      Burrell, Black Stars, 2:32-39, Dec. 1972.

259. "Hollywood's new Black beauties, " Sepia, 22:37-44,
      March 1973.
            (Lola Falana, Brenda Sykes, Cicely Tyson, Diana
            Ross, Mae Mercer, Kathy Imrie, Paula Kelly,
            Rosalind Cash, Vonetta McGee, Freda Payne, Diana
            Sands, Lisa Moore, Denise Nicholas, Judy Pace,
            Margaret Ware.)

260. "Is Hollywood afraid to star a sexy actress?" Sepia,
      18:10-15, June 1969.

261. "The passing of Beulah: will Hattie McDaniel's death
      mark end of long era of 'Kitchen-Comedy' roles for
      Negroes on radio and screen?" Our World, 8:12-15,
      Feb. 1953.

262. "The tattered queens; some reflections on the Negro
      actress, " Ruby Dee, Negro Digest, 15:32-36, April
      1966.

THE BLACK "BOOM"

263. "The Black boom, " Liberator, 4:16₊, Aug. 1964.

(Discussion of <u>Black Like Me</u> and <u>The Cool World.</u>)

264.   "Black Hollywood: out of the movie kitchen and into
       society and the money, " <u>Life</u> (Movies) Jan. 23, 1970,
       pp. M19-M21.

265.   "Black market, " <u>Time</u>, 99:53, April 10, 1972.

266.   "Black movie boom, " <u>Newsweek</u>, 78:66, Sept. 6, 1971.

267.   "Black movies: renaissance or ripoff?" <u>Newsweek</u>,
       80:74-8, Oct. 23, 1972.

268.   "Black pic cycle mushrooming, " <u>Daily Variety</u>, 157:1,
       Sept. 14, 1972.

269.   "The boom is really an echo, " <u>Black Creation</u>, 4:32-
       34, Winter 1973.

270.   "A flood of Black films, " <u>Essence</u>, 5:28, Sept. 1972.
       ("A few years ago there was scarcely a Black film.
       Now there are more and more because of the Black
       film fad. ")

271.   "Griffin backs out of Blaxploitation coalition post, "
       <u>Daily Variety</u>, Aug. 1, 1972.

272.   "New films: culture or con game?" <u>Ebony</u>, 28:60-2,
       Dec. 1972.

273.   "Raymond St. Jacques claims critics pamper Black
       films, " Ron Pennington, <u>Hollywood Reporter</u>, Jan. 8,
       1973, p. 13.

COMMENTS AND CRITICISM

274.   "ABC's of movieland, " Gertrude Gipson, <u>Our World</u>,
       7:60-64, Sept. 1952.

275.   "Beige, brown, or black, " Albert Johnson, <u>Film
       Quarterly</u>, 13:38-43, Fall 1959.
       (Analysis of filmdom's approach to interracialism,
       which is characterized as "vague, inconclusive, and
       undiscussed, ")

276. "The Birth of a Nation, " Crisis, 14:25-26, May 1917.

277. "Birth of a Nation, " New Republic, 2:185, Mar. 20,
      1915.

278. "Black and white: The screen, " Colin L. Westerbeck,
      Jr. Commonweal, 96:285-6, May 26, 1972.
      (Critique of the Black films Georgia, Georgia, Buck
      and the Preacher, and Cool Breeze.)

279. "Black film: God's step children, " New Yorker, 46:
      34-35, Apr. 18, 1970.

280. "Black films: values, pro and con, " Senior Scholastic,
      101:8-10, Dec. 11, 1972.

281. "Blacks vs. Shaft, " Newsweek, 80:88, Aug. 28, 1972.

282. "Celebrity marriages; stars overcome odds with love,"
      Gertrude Gipson, Los Angeles Sentinel, Sept. 20, 1973,
      p. A1.
      (Such stars as Dionne Warwicke, Bill Elliot; Judy
      Pace, Don Mitchell; Paula Kelly, Bernie Casey.)

283. "Clayton Riley on the Black critic, " Black Creation,
      3:15, Summer 1972.

284. "Dark laughter, " Time,   18, 35:84, April 29, 1940.
      (Critique of movie Mister Washington Goes to
      Town.)

285. "Enroute to the future, " Negro History Bulletin, 30:
      13, April 1967.

286. "Expanding world of the Black film (editorial), " Black
      Creation, 4:25, Winter 1973.

287. "Films for Blacks, " Richard Schickel, Life, 72:20,
      June 1972.
      (Reviews of Buck and the Preacher, Nigger Charley,
      Soul Soldier, and Cool Breeze.)

288. "A futuristic fable, " Black Creation, 4:43, Winter
      1973.

289. "Hollywood in glorious Black and white, " Leonard
      Feather, Entertainment World, Dec. 12, 1969.

290. "Hollywood ... so what!" Our World, 8:56-59, Dec.
      1953.
            (James Edwards says you must not believe every-
            thing you hear about Hollywood.)

291. "Hollywood's boy and girl next door--color them white,"
      Lindsay Patterson, New York Times, June 16, 1968,
      p. D9.

292. "Hollywood's new Negro films, " Loren Miller, Crisis,
      45:8, Jan. 1938.

293. "How liberal is show business?" Sepia, 12:40-43,
      March 1963.

294. "If Poitier can't do it they rewrite for a white actor:
      Bill Gunn's beef, " Robert B. Frederick, Variety
      Weekly, Oct. 4, 1964.

295. "It could only happen in jolly Hollywood, " Cinemeditor,
      Fall, 1970, pp. 8-18+.

296. "More about Black films, " America, 127:459-60,
      November 25, 1972.

297. "Negro actors should act, not be diverted, says Yaphet
      Kotto, " Hollywood Reporter, June 4, 1968.
            (Kotto is quoted as saying he is "tired of hearing
            actors talking about social revolution when, instead
            they should be concentrating on what they have to
            do when they go on stage or before a camera. ")

298. "The Negro and the movies, " Negro Digest, 1:19-21,
      April 1943.

299. "New look in Hollywood, " Sepia, 7:30-34, Mar. 1959.

300. "Notes on Black movies, " New Yorker, 48:159-65,
      Dec. 2, 1972.

301. "Otto Preminger on Black movies, " Encore, 2:56-59,
      Aug. 1973.

302. "Prejudicial film: progress and stalemate (1915-
      1967), " Phylon. 31:142-7, Summer 1970.

303. "Secular prophecy in an age of film, " Journal of

Religious Thought,   27:63-75, Spring-Summer 1970.

304. "So now I'm back, and Black ... and available, " Peter
DeAnda, New York Times, Oct. 10, 1971.
("Lament" on the fact that "Black" is going out of
style in Hollywood.)

305. "The sound track, " [Column] William Mooring, New
York Tidings, June 2, 1944.

306. "Sportin' Life and the strange 'lady', " Ebony, 14:97-
98, Feb. 1959.

307. "Stanley Kaufmann on films, " New Republic, 167: 20+,
April 28, 1973.

308. "The ten most important Black films between 1962 and
1972 [list], " Black Creation, Win. 1973.

309. "Two social scientists view No Way Out; the unconscious vs. the message in an anti-bias film, " Commentary, 10:388-91, Oct. 1950.
(Martha Wolfenstein and Nathan Leites.)

310. "Violence overdone in Black capers?" Robert B.
Frederick, Variety Weekly, Mar. 7, 1973.

311. "West coast gets the Shaft, " Black Creation, 3:12-14,
Summer 1972.

312. "What's cookin' in Hollywood?" Our World, 7:62-63,
Oct. 1952.

313. "Why does white America love Sidney Poitier so?"
Clifford Mason, New York Times, Sept. 10, 1967. p. 1.

314. "Why the stars go broke. " Ebony, 18:84-88, July 1963.
(The cases of Dorothy Dandridge, Stepin Fetchit,
Ethel Waters and others.)

FILM AND BLACK ATHLETES

315. "Actor Satch: ageless hurler plays cavalry sergeant, "
Ebony, 15:109-110, Dec. 1959.

(Satchel Paige.)

316.   "Aftermath: Here is Marva ... " Our World, 8:12-13,
        July 1953.
        (Choosing of Hilda Simms to play role of Marva
        Louis in The Joe Louis Story.)

317.   "Althea's film debut, " Ebony, 14:73-74, July 1959.
        (Althea Gibson.)

318.   "Athlete Rafer Johnson becomes top Hollywood star, "
        Sepia, 11:58-62, June 1962.

319.   "Canada Lee back in ring: ex-pug makes comeback in
        boxing and in films, " Ebony, 2:16-17, Aug. 1947.
        (In movie Body and Soul.)

320.   "Football heroes invade Hollywood, " Ebony, 24:195-
        197, Oct. 1969.

321.   "Great athlete finds Hollywood stardom, " Sepia, 8:64-
        67, Aug. 1960.
        (Woody Strode.)

322.   "Harder They Fall, Joe Walcott is convincing actor in
        first movie role, " Ebony, 11:87-90, May 1956.

323.   "Jackie Robinson Story: new movie tells story of first
        Negro in big league baseball, " Ebony, 5:87-88+, June
        1950.

324.   "Karate champion Jim Kelly makes movie debut, "
        Los Angeles Sentinel, Sept. 6, 1973, p. B2A.

325.   "Rafer Johnson: born to be a star, " Sepia, 19:30-32,
        Feb, 1970.

326.   "A superstar in Maurie: Bernie Casey, " Los Angeles
        Sentinel, Sept. 6, 1973, p. B1A.

327.   "Why I played Jim, the slave, " Archie Moore, Ebony,
        15:43-44+, Sept. 1960.

328.   "Willie Davis: baseball player, natural actor, " Sepia,
        19:58-63, May 1970.

BLACK MUSICIANS AND MUSIC

329. "Anatomy of a Murder: Hollywood uses talents of Duke
      Ellington in movie, " Ebony, 14:106-108, Sept. 1959.

330. "Crooner Nat King Cole turns actor, " Ebony, 12:74,
      June 1957.

331. "High Society: new movie with jazz angle has role made
      for Satchmo, " Ebony, 11:103-105, July 1956.

332. "Hollywood and the Negro musician" [advertisement],
      Henry Roth, Daily Variety, Feb. 17, 1964. p. 12.
          (The leading Hollywood Negro musicians ... do not
          want any concessions because they are Negro. They
          only want to compete on a fair and equal basis.)

333. "Mahalia swings again, " Sepia, 13:42-45, Mar. 1964.
          (Mahalia Jackson in film The Best Man.)

334. "Movie choir: mixed Hairston Chorus of 17 voices has
      done music for 40 films, " Ebony, 4:25-27, Oct. 1949.
          (The Jester Hairston Choir.)

335. "Movie musicals; ranking Negro performers given
      musical bits in half-dozen coming Hollywood produc-
      tions, " Ebony, 6:51-53, Aug. 1951.

336. "Of Men and Music: story of Marian Anderson is told
      in music film series, " Ebony, 6:49-50+, May 1951.

337. "Pete Kelly's Blues, Ella Fitzgerald draws a hot jazz
      assignment for her first major role in movies, " Ebony,
      1:115-117, Oct. 1955.

338. "St. Louis Blues, Nat King Cole plays lead role in film
      biography of W. C. Handy, " Ebony, 13:27-28, May 1958.

339. "Take a Giant Step: singer Johnny Nash makes debut
      as an actor, " Ebony, 14:48-51, Sept. 1959.

340. "Worthwhile music in the movies; much choral work by
      Negro organization, " Etude, 57:152, March 1939. Verna
      Arvey.
          (Negro choral groups working on movies in Holly-
          wood.)

ACTORS AND ACTRESSES

341. BAILEY, PEARL
        "Hollywood debut for Pearl Bailey, " Ebony, 2:38-
        39, April 1947.

342.   "The Pearl Bailey nobody knows, " Doris Black,
          Sepia, 20:54-61, April 1971.

343.   "A pooped Pearlie Mae," Ebony, 13:55-56, Apr.
          1958.

344. BEARD, MATTHEW, JR.
        "I wish mom could see me now, " Skip Ferderber,
        Los Angeles Times, Nov. 22, 1973, Part 4, p. 36.
        (Matthew Beard, Jr., who played the role of
        Stymie in the Our Gang comedies.)

345. BELAFONTE, HARRY
        "Belafonte: 'Look, ' they tell me, 'don't rock the
        boat, ' " Harry Belafonte, New York Times, April
        21, 1968.

346.   "Island in the Sun: Dandridge, Belafonte star in
          romantic interracial film, " Ebony, 12:32-34+,
          July 1957.

347.   "Poitier meets Belafonte, " George Goodman. Look,
          35:56-60, Aug. 24, 1971.
          (Review of Buck and the Preacher.)

348. BLACKMAN, DON
        "Don Blackman's big role in Santiago, " Color, 11:
        7-9, Aug. 1956.

349. BROWN, JIM
        "Jim Brown in Rio Conchos, " Sepia, 13:22-25,
        Dec. 1964.

350.   "Jim Brown may make it in pics, à la Poitier, "
          Variety Weekly, Jan. 24, 1968.

351.   "No color line in casting: (Jim) Brown and Raquel
          Welch, " Film-TV Daily, May 24, 1968.

352. CARROLL, DIAHANN

"Diahann Carroll: talented bombshell, " Sepia, 11:
57-59, Mar. 1962.

353.   "Sidney Poitier-Diahann Carroll: what will it be?"
Sepia, 14:8-12+, June 1965.

354. CASEY, BERNIE
"A super star in Maurie: multitalented Bernie
Casey emerges, " Los Angeles Sentinel, Sept. 6,
1973, p. B1A.

355. CLARKE, ALEX
"Talented Alex Clarke is a bold Black actor, "
Pittsburgh Courier, Jan. 10, 1970, p. 12.
(Star of The Learning Tree.)

356. COLE, CAROL
"Nat Cole's daughter seeks movie stardom, " Sepia,
15:32-37, June 1966.

357. COMFORT, MADI
"Madi Comfort: newest movie queen, " Ebony, 10:
25-28, Sept. 1955.

358. CONNOR, EDRIC
"Moby Dick: Calypso singer Edric Connor plays
choice role in adventurous film about whaling men,"
Ebony, 10:107-109, Sept. 1955.

359. DANDRIDGE, DOROTHY
"Can Dandridge outshine Lena Horne?" Our World,
7:29-32, June 1952.

360.   "Dandridge gets red carpet treatment, " Ebony, 11:
24, Aug. 1956.

361.   "Dandridge marries: simple wedding is movieland
wonder, " Ebony, 14:135-138, Sept. 1959.

362.   "Decks ran red: in eighth movie, Dorothy Dandridge displays acting skill, " Ebony, 14:60-62, Nov.
1958.

363.   "Dorothy Dandridge's death recalls efforts to expand
scope of roles for Negroes, " Variety Weekly,
Sept. 15, 1965.

364.   "Dorothy Dandridge's greatest triumph, " Ebony,
         10:37-41, July 1955.

365.   "Grace through exercise, " Ebony, 14:33-36, March
         1959.

366.   "Island in the Sun: Dandridge, Belafonte star in
         romantic interracial film, " Ebony, 12:32-34+, July
         1957.

367.   "Life and death of Dorothy Dandridge, " A. S.
         Young, Sepia, 14:8-12+, Dec. 1965.

368.   "Private world of Dorothy Dandridge, " Ebony, 17:
         116-121, June 1962.

369.   "Screen test; Dorothy Dandridge wins Carmen Jones
         title role with sizzling performance, " Ebony, 9:37-
         40, Sept. 1954.

370. DAVIS, OSSIE
         "Negroes still given racially oriented pic roles:
         O. Davis, " Allen Lobsenz, Film Daily, Oct. 11,
         1965.

371. DIXON, IVAN
         "Ivan Dixon at home, " Sepia, 16:38-41, February
         1967.

372.   "Many faces of Ivan Dixon, " Sepia, 14:32-36, July
         1965.

373. EDWARDS, JAMES
         "Hollywood: so what!" Our World, 8:56-59, Dec.
         1953.
              (Comments by James Edwards.)

374.   "Movie debut: ex-G.I. James Edwards passes first
         film test with help of star Robert Ryan's advice.
         Ebony, 4:25, April 1949.

375.   "Sad semi-secret death of a star: James Edwards's
         death goes almost unnoticed by those he helped, "
         Sepia, 19:72-77, Mar. 1970.

376. FALANA, LOLA
         "Whatever Lola wants, Lola Falana gets, " Sepia,

16:32-36, Apr. 1967.

377. FIEGERT, ELFIE
"Negro actors win roles in German films and television; orphan to star at 17," Elfie Fiegert, Variety Weekly, July 31, 1963.

378. FRANCIS, VERA
"President's Lady: Vera Francis gets explosive role
in movie touching on mixed romance theme," Ebony,
8:71-75, Feb. 1953.

379.   "Vera Francis; movies' new sex thrill," Our
World, 8:54-57, March 1953.

380. GRIER, PAM
"Pam Grier is Foxy Brown," Los Angeles Sentinel,
Oct. 11, 1973, P. b6.

381. HARRIS, DARRELL
"A star at ten: cub scout gets featured role in
Tarzan film," Ebony, 13:59, July 1958.
(Darrell Harris in Tarzan's Fight for Life.)

382. HENDRY, GLORIA
"The Black girl who plays the wife of James Bond,"
Sepia, 22:35-42, May 1973.
(Gloria Hendry.)

383. HERNANDEZ, JUANO
"From actor to college prof: movie star Juano
Hernandez returns to native Puerto Rico for teach-
ing job," Ebony, 8:122-126, Nov. 1952.

384.   "Trial: cast as a judge, actor Juano Hernandez is
given best role of his Hollywood career," Ebony,
11:29-30+, Nov. 1955.

385. HORNE, LENA
"Can Dandridge outshine Lena Horne?" Our World,
7:29-32, June 1952.

386.   "Lena Horne speaks freely on race, marriage,
stage," Robert Feinstein, Ebony, 18:61-67, May
1963.

387.   "Tooting Lena's horn," Charlotte Kay, Negro

Digest, 3:25-29, Aug. 1945.

388. INGRAM, REX
"'De Lawd' cooks with gas, "   Negro Digest,   2:53-
55, Jan. 1944.

389.   "I came back from the dead, "   Ebony,   10:49-52,
March, 1955.

390. JONES, JAMES EARL
"James Earl Jones: actor still climbing, "   Ebony,
20:98-106, April 1965.

391.   "James Earl Jones' goal is to become great actor,"
Sepia, 13:72-76, Feb. 1964.

392.   "James Earl Jones: race is still the important
thing, "   Sepia, 20:16-17, Jan. 1971.

393.   "Sudden stardom for James Earl Jones, "   Sepia,
18:52-55, June 1969.

394.   "Young actor on the way up: James Earl Jones, "
Robert Burg, Negro Digest, 15:26-31, Apr. 1966.

395. KELLY, JIM
"Karate champion Jim Kelly makes movie debut, "
Los Angeles Sentinel, Sept. 6, 1973, p. B2A.

396. KITT, EARTHA
"Why Negroes don't like Eartha Kitt, "   Ebony, 10:
29-38, Dec. 1954.

397. KOTTO, YAPHET
"Negro actors should act, not be diverted, says
Yaphet Kotto, "   Hollywood Reporter, June 4, 1968.

398. LOURANT, ARTHUR "CHICO"
"Yank movie man of Japan: virile American actor
Chico-san wins wide popularity in fast action Japanese movies, radio and television shows, "   Ebony,
18:45-46+, July 1963.
    (Arthur "Chico" Lourant.)

399. McDANIEL, HATTIE
"The passing of Beulah, "   Our World, 8:12-15,
Feb. 1953.

400.   MACLACHLAN, JANET
       "Janet Maclachlan grabs filmland's brass ring, "
       Sepia, 19:54-58, Mar. 70.

401.   McNAIR, BARBARA
       "Barbara McNair: the acting debut of a singer, "
       Sepia, 13:74-78, Apr. 64.

402.   "Beauty that is Barbara McNair, " Sepia, 19:72-73,
       Nov. 1970.

403.   MARSHALL, WILLIAM
       "Bill Marshall: matinee idol, " Our World, 9:38-41,
       Feb. 1954.

404.   "Black actor William Marshall gives pedagogs low-
       down on 'coon' age, " Lee Beaupre, Variety Weekly,
       Aug. 15, 1973.

405.   MILLS, ALLISON
       "Allison Mills: image of Hollywood's new breed, "
       W. Jenkins, Sepia, 19:14-17, July 1970.

406.   MOORE, JUANITA
       "Imitation of Life: Juanita Moore stars in new ver-
       sion of film, " Ebony, 14:70-73, Apr. 1959.

407.   MOORE, TOMMIE
       "Movie features blossoming star, " Ebony,   13:93-
       94, Nov. 1957.

408.   O'NEAL, RON
       "O'Neal defends Superfly, " Daily Variety, 157:1,
       Sept. 14, 1972.

409.   PACE, JUDY
       "Teenagers win movie roles, " Ebony, 18:150-152,
       May 1963.

410.   PARKS, TRINA
       "Trina Parks: the girl who zaps James Bond, "
       Ebony, 27:68-70, Mar. 1972.

411.   PETERS, BROCK
       "Brock Peters, " Ebony, 18:106-112, June 1963.

412.   "This may be year industry makes itself clear as

far as Negro is concerned, says Brock Peters, "
<u>Hollywood Reporter</u>, Feb. 12, 1968.

413.   PETERSON, CALEB
       "<u>Any Number Can Play</u>: Caleb Peterson gets excel-
       lent part in new Clark Gable starrer, " <u>Ebony</u>, 4:
       24-26, May 1949.

414.   POITIER, SIDNEY
       "<u>Blackboard Jungle</u>: Sidney Poitier has key role in
       brutal film about teacher, juvenile delinquents, "
       <u>Ebony</u>,   14:100-103, May 1959.

415.   "Expanding world of Sidney Poitier, " L. Robinson,
       <u>Ebony</u>,   27:1-11+, Nov. 1971.

416.   "Films, Poitier, and race riots, " Robert J.
       Landry, <u>Variety Weekly</u>, Jan. 3, 1968, p. 12.

417.   "Hollywood's first Negro movie star: Sidney Poitier
       breaks film barrier to become screen idol, "
       Lerone Bennett, Jr. , <u>Ebony</u>, 14:100-103, May 1959.

418.   "How Sidney Poitier won an Oscar, " <u>Sepia</u>, 13:14-
       17, June 1964.

419.   "The Negro in films: Poitier points a dilemma
       which <u>The Cool World</u> helps rebut, " <u>New York
       Times</u>, Apr. 26, 1964.

420.   "Poitier meets Belafonte, " George Goodman, <u>Look</u>,
       35:56-60, Aug. 24, 1971.
       (Review of <u>Buck and the Preacher</u>.)

421.   "Sidney Poitier-Diahann Carroll, " <u>Sepia</u>, 14:8-12+,
       June, 1965.

422.   "Sidney Poitier makes relevant film for Blacks, "
       C. S. Thompson, <u>Jet</u>, 41:58-61, May 13, 1971.

423.   "Sidney Poitier: the man behind the star, " C. L.
       Sanders, <u>Ebony</u>, 23:172-174+, Apr. 68.

424.   "Sidney Poitier's fight with a Nazi, " <u>Sepia</u>, 11:41-
       44, Sept. 1962.

425.   "Straight with no cop-outs, " <u>Social Problems</u>, 16:

525-527, Spring 1969.
(Analysis of Guess Who's Coming to Dinner and Patch of Blue.)

426.   "Why does white America love Sidney Poitier so?" Clifford Mason, New York Times, Sept. 10, 67, p. 1.

427.   "Why I became an actor," Negro Digest, 11:80-97, Dec. 1961.
(Sidney Poitier.)

428.   PRENDERGAST, TESSA
"Movie starlet's Roman holiday: Jamaica-born beauty finds fun, romance while awaiting fame in Italian capital," Ebony, 10:27-30+, Jan. 1955.

429.   RAWLS, LOU
"Lou Rawls stars in first all-Black cowboy movie," Collette Wood, Hollywood Reporter, Sept. 17, 1969.

430.   de RIVEL, MOUNE
"French movie star: Moune de Rivel, onetime cafe society singer, stars in new film touching on racial bias," Ebony, 8:103-108, Mar. 1953.

431.   ROBESON, PAUL
"Paul Robeson and Black identity in American films," Massachusetts Review, 11:468-85, Summer 1970.

432.   "Return of the Emperor Jones," Negro History Bulletin, 34:160-162, Nov. 1971.

433.   "Tribute to Paul Robeson," Film Culture, Fall, Winter 1970.

434.   ROSAMOND, PATRICIA
"A Star Is Born," Ebony, 10:90-94, Jan. 1955.

435.   ROSS, DIANA
"Lady Sings the Blues, Diana Ross sweeps top award Venice Festival," Los Angeles Sentinel, Oct. 4, 1973, p. B1B.

436.   ROUNDTREE, RICHARD
"From model to movie star," Ebony, 26:128, June 1971.

437.   "MGM creates a Black star: first in 60 years, "
            Norfolk Journal and Guide, Apr. 10, 1971, p. 14.

438.   SAILES, BOBBY
            "A Star Is Born, " Ebony, 10:90-94, Jan. 1955.

439.   ST. JACQUES, RAYMOND
            "New bad guy of the movies: actor teams with Liz
            Taylor, Richard Burton in film blast aimed at Haiti
            dictatorship, " Charles L. Sanders, Ebony, 22:171-
            172+, June 1967.

440.   "Raymond St. Jacques claims critics pamper Black
            films, " Ron Pennington, Hollywood Reporter, Jan.
            8, 1973, p. 13.

441.   "Raymond St. Jacques: a new meaning for 'super-
            star', " Sepia, 19:62-65, Aug. 1970.

442.   "Raymond the magnificent, " Charles L. Sanders,
            Ebony, 25:175-178+, Nov. 1969.

443.   STEPIN FETCHIT
            "Stepin Fetchit comes back, " Ebony, 7:64-67, Feb.
            1952.

444.   "Stepin Fetchit talks back, " (interview), Film
            Quarterly, 24:20-26, Summer 1971.

445.   STRODE, WOODY
            "Strode is brilliant as 'Black Jesus', " Jet, 41:53,
            Oct. 7, 1971.

446.   "Woody Strode does it again, " Sepia, 14:18-21,
            Aug. 1965.

447.   SUL-TE-WAN, MME.
            "Mme. Sul-Te-Wan: at 80, she's the oldest Negro
            actress in Hollywood, " Our World, 9:80-82, Feb.
            1954.

448.   TYSON, CICELY
            "Cicely Tyson, " Time, 100:58, Oct. 9, 1972.

449.   WALKER, BILL
            "Jamaica Sea, " Our World, 7:60-61, Dec. 1952.

450. WARFIELD, WILLIAM
      "Showboat: William Warfield makes film debut in
      revival, " Ebony, 6:69-71, Jan. 1951.

451. WATERS, ETHEL
      "Member of the wedding: Ethel Waters, " Ebony,
      8:47-51, Dec. 1952.

452.   "Miss Waters' regrets, " Ebony, 8:47-51, Dec.
      1952.

453.   "Three lives of Ethel Waters, " Reader's Digest,
      101:81-85, Dec. 1972.

454. WILLIAMS, BILLY
      "Rebel with a cause: new lease on life for Billy
      Williams, " Sepia, 9:37-41, Mar. 1960.

455. WILLIAMSON, FRED
      "Hell up in Harlem stars Fred Williamson, " Los
      Angeles Sentinel, Oct. 11, 1973, p. B7.

456. WINFIELD, PAUL
      "Paul Winfield: a man unto himself, " Essence,
      4:27+, June 1973.

MOVIES

457. "All the Young Men, " Ebony, 15:83-84+, Aug. 1960.

458. "All the Young Men, " Sepia, 8:56-61, June 1960.

459. "Anatomy of a Murder, " Ebony, 14:106-108, Sept.
      1959.

460. "Ancient film's effect on modern Negro life, " Los
      Angeles Times, Feb. 15, 1965.
      (The Birth of a Nation.)

461. "Androcles and the Lion, " Ebony, 7:39-42+, Aug.
      1952.

462. "Angelitos Negros, " Crisis, 57:221-225+, Apr. 1950.

463.   "Angelitos Negros, " Ebony, 5:48-50, Feb. 1950.

464.   "Anna Lucasta: Eartha Kitt, Sammy Davis star in
       film, " Ebony, 14:72-76, Dec. 1958.

465.   "Anna's Sin, " Ebony, 9:33-36, March 1953.

466.   "Anna's Sin, " Sepia, 10:38-40, May 1961.

467.   "Any Number Can Play, " Ebony, 4:24-26, May 1949.

468.   "Balcony, " Sepia, 12:64-65, April 1963.

469.   "Band of Angels, " Ebony, 12:58-61, Sept. 1957.

470.   "Benny Goodman Story, " Ebony, 11:77-80, Feb. 1956.

471.   "The Birth of a Nation, " Crisis, 14:25-26, May 1917.

472.   "The Birth of a Nation, " Los Angeles Times, Feb.
       15, 1965.

473.   "The Birth of a Nation, " New Republic, 2:185, March
       20, 1915.

474.   "The Birth of a Nation, " Peter Noble, Sight and
       Sound, Fall 1946.

475.   "Director Ossie Davis talks about Black Girl, " Black
       Creation, 4:38-39, Winter 1973.

476.   "Black Gold, " Ebony, 2:39, Oct. 1947.

477.   "Black Klansman, " Sepia, 15:64-67, June 1966.

478.   "Black Like Me, " Ebony, 19:37-38+, May 1964.

479.   "Blackboard Jungle: Sidney Poitier has key role in
       brutal film about teacher, juvenile delinquents, " Ebony,
       10:87-88, May 1955.

480.   "Body and Soul, " Ebony, 2:16-17, Aug. 1947.

481.   "Breaking Point, " Our World, 5:51, Aug. 1950.

482.   "The Burning Cross, " Ebony, 2:36-41, Sept. 1947.

483. "Buck and the Preacher," Essence, 3:8, Aug. 1972.

484. "The Cardinal," Ebony, 19:126-128+, Dec. 1963.

485. "Carmen Jones," Collier's, 113:14-15.

486. "Carmen Jones' box office click improves Negro cast-
      ing chances," Variety Weekly, Feb. 23, 1955.

487. "Screen test; Dorothy Dandridge wins Carmen Jones
      title role with sizzling performance," Ebony, 9:37-
      40, Sept. 1954.

488. "A Child Waits," Ebony, 18:89-90+, March 63.

489. "China Gate," Ebony, 12:74+, June 1957.

490. "Cool World," Ebony, 20:43-44+, July 1965.

491. "The Cool World," New York Times, Apr. 26, 1964.

492. "Cotton Comes to Harlem," Black Theatre, 47-49,
      1971.

493. "Crowning Experience," Sepia, 9:20-22, Feb. 1961.

494. "Cruisin' Down the River," Our World, 8:32-33, Jun.
      1953.

495. "Cry the Beloved Country," Ebony, 6:57-62, Jul. 1951.

496. "Dark horse operas: a film article," Negro History
      Bulletin, 36:13-14, Ja. 1973.
         (Black Westerns.)

497. "Deep Is the Well," Ebony, 6:38-42, Feb. 1951.

498. "Defiant Ones," Ebony, 13:80-82+, Oct. 1958.

499. "Demetrius and the Gladiators," Ebony, 9:91-94,
      Nov. 1953.

500. "Detective Story," Ebony, !, 95-98, Dec. 1951.

501. "Diary of Anne Frank," Ebony, 14:57-59, June 1959.

502. "Edge of the City," Ebony, 12:75-76+, May 1957.

503. "The Egyptian," Ebony, 9:83-86, Aug. 1954.

504. "Return of the Emperor Jones," Negro History Bulletin, 34:160-2, Nov. 1971.

505. "Foxy Brown," Los Angeles Sentinel, Oct. 11, 1973, p. B6.

506. "The Gladiators," Our World, 8:8+, Oct. 1953.

507. "Globe Trotters," Our World, 6:40-44, Apr. 1951.

508. "Glory Alley," Ebony, 7:100-102+, May 1952.

509. "Go for Broke," Crisis, 60:17-19, Jan. 1953.

510. "Great White Hope," Jet, 39:58, Feb. 25, 1971.

511. "The Great White Hope," Gary Arnold, Washington Post, December 31, 1970, p. C1.

512. "G'wan with the Wind," New Masses, 34:28, Jan. 2, 1940.
         (Gone with the Wind.)

513. "Green Mansions," Ebony, 13:121-122, Oct. 1958.

514. "The Green Pastures," Time, #26, 27:38-40, Jun. 29, 1936.

515. "The Green Pastures again," Doris B. Garey, Phylon, 20:193-194, Summer 1959.

516. "How genuine is The Green Pastures?" Nick Aaron Ford, Phylon, 20:67-70, Spring 1959.

517. "A modern miracle play--Green Pastures," Euphemia V. R. Wyatt, Catholic World, 131:210-11, May 1930.

518. "Guess Who's Coming to Dinner," Ebony, 23:56-58+, Jan. 1968.

519. "Guns at Batasi," Sepia, 13:16-19, Nov. 1964.

520. "Hallelujah," Time, 14:64, Sept. 2, 1929.

521. "Hearts in Dixie," Opportunity, 7:122-123, Apr. 1929.

522. "Hell up in Harlem, " Los Angeles Sentinel, Oct. 11, 1973, p. B7.

523. "High Society, " Ebony, 14:70-73, April 1959.

524. "Hole in the Head, " Ebony, 14:83-84₊, Aug. 1959.

525. "Home of the Brave, " Ebony, 4:59-62, June 1949.

526. "Horse Soldiers, " Ebony, 14:73-74₊, July 1959.

527. "End of a controversy" [Imitation of Life], Sterling A. Brown, Opportunity, #8, 13:231, August 1935.

528. "Imitation of Life, Juanita Moore stars in new version of film, " Ebony, 14:70-73, Apr. 1959.

529. "The Intruder, " Ebony, 17:76-79, May 1962.

530. "Intruder in the Dust, " Ebony, 4:25-28, Aug. 1949.

531. "Island in the Sun, " Ebony, 12:32-34₊, July 1957.

532. "It's your Thing, " Washington Post, Sept. 3, 1970, p. C22.

533. "Jackie Robinson Story, " Ebony, 5:87-88₊, June 1950.

534. "Jackie Robinson Story, " Our World, 5:36-38, June 1950.

535. "Jedda, " Ebony, 12:108₊, Mar. 1957.

536. "Khartoum, " Negro Digest, 16:32-36₊, Feb. 1967.

537. "Kings Go Forth, " Sepia, 6:65-69, May 1958.

538. "Kisses for My President, " New York Times, Sept. 22, 1963.

539. "Kisses for My President, " Wall Street Journal, Sept. 24, 1963.

540. "Knock on Any Door, " Ebony, 4:34-38, Jan. 1949.

541. "Kongi's Harvest, " Sepia, 20:59-63, Sept. 1971.

542. "Lady Sings the Blues, " Los Angeles Sentinel, Oct. 4,
      1973, p. B1A.

543. "Last Angry Man, " Ebony, 15:42-44, Jan. 1960.

544. "Lawless, " Ebony, 5:59-62, May, 1950.

545. "The Learning Tree, " Sepia, 19:50-52+, Apr. 1970.

546. "Let No Man Write My Epitaph, " Ebony, 15:94-96+,
      Oct. 1960.

547. "Lights Out, " Ebony, 6:87-88+, Dec. 1950.

548. "Lilies of the Field, " Ebony, 18:55-58, Oct. 1963.

549. "Lost Boundaries, " Ebony, 4:51-53, July 1949.

550. "Lydia Bailey, " Ebony, 7:39-44, Jan. 1952.

551. "Lydia Bailey, " Our World, 6:12-14, Dec. 1951.

552. "Lydia Bailey, " Our World, 7:46-53, Aug. 1952.

553. "Mambo, " Ebony, 10:83-84+, Dec. 1954.

554. "Man and Boy, " Ebony, 26:42-44+, Apr. 1971.

555. "Maurie, " Los Angeles Sentinel, Sept. 6, 1973, p. B1A.

556. "Member of the Wedding: Ethel Waters, " Ebony, 8:47-
      51, Dec. 1952.

557. "Member of the Wedding, " Our World, 7:59-61, Oct.
      1952.

558. "Moby Dick, " Ebony, 10:107-109, Sept. 1955.

559. "Moby Dick, " Our World, 10:62-64, June 1955.

560. "Moulin Rouge, " Our World, 8:8+, Mar. 1953.

561. "Mulatto, " Crisis, 57:698-699, Dec. 1950.

562. "Mulatto, " Our World, 6:50, Jan. 1951.

563. "Naked Maja, " Ebony, 14:103-105, Feb. 1959.

564. "Naked Prey, " Sepia, 15:66-70, Dec. 1966.

565. "Native Son, " Our World, 5:36-38, Dec. 1950.

566. "Native Son filmed in Argentina, " Ebony, 6:82-86,
      Jan. 1951.

567. "Negro playwright's classic becomes a movie, " Sepia,
      7:57-62, Apr. 1959.
            (Take a giant step.)

568. "No Way Out, " Ebony, 5:31-34, Mar. 1950.

569. "No Way Out, " Our World, 5:32-33, Apr. 1950.

570. "None But the Brave, " Ebony, 19:110-112+, Oct. 1964.

571. "Nothing But a Man, " Ebony, 20:198-201, Apr. 1965.

572. "Nothing But a Man, " Negro Digest, 14:49, May 1965.

573. "Odds Against Tomorrow, " Ebony, 15:68-70+, Nov.
      1959.

574. "Of Men and Music, " Ebony, 6:49-50+, May 1951.

575. "Do you remember Our Gang?" Negro Digest, 9:69-
      70, Dec. 1950.

576. "Our Man in Havana, " Ebony, 15:66+, Mar. 1960.

577. "Panic in the Streets, " Our World, 5:47, Nov. 1950.

578. "Paris Blues, " Ebony, 16:46-50, Aug. 1961.

579. "The Peanut Man, " Ebony, 2:48-50, July 1947.

580. "Pinky, " Ebony, 4:23-25, Sept. 1949.

581. "Pool of London, " Ebony, 6:59-61, Oct. 1951.

582. "Pool of London, " Our World, 6:43-45, Sept. 1951.

583. "Boycott in Hollywood?" [Porgy & Bess] Time, 70:
      90, Dec. 2, 1959.

584. "Sepia goes to premier of Porgy and Bess, " Sepia,

7:8-14, Sept. 1959.

585. "Why Negroes don't like Porgy and Bess," Ebony, 14: 50-52, Oct. 1952.

586. "Pressure Point," Ebony, 18:45-46+, Nov. 1962.

587. "Prisoner of War," Ebony, 9:77-80+, June 1954.

588. "Raisin in the Sun," Ebony, 16:53-56+, Apr. 1961.

589. "Red Ball Express," Ebony, 7:51-54, June 1952.

590. "Red Ball Express," Our World, 7:42-43, Apr. 1952.

591. "Rio Conchos," Sepia, 13:22-25, Dec. 1964.

592. "Robin and the Seven Hoods," Ebony, 19:90-92+, June 1964.

593. "Santiago," Color, 11:7-9, Aug. 1956.

594. "Sapphire," Ebony, 15:51-54+, Dec. 1959.

595. "Save the Children," Los Angeles Sentinel, Oct. 25, 1973. p. B9.

596. "See How They Run," Our World, 7:10+, Nov. 1952.

597. "Sergeant Rutledge," Ebony, 15:15-76+, July 1960.

598. "Shaft," Crisis, 78:162, July 1971.

599. "Shaft," Essence, 2:76, Aug. 1971.

600. "Showboat: William Warfield makes film debut in revival," Ebony, 6:69-71, Jan. 1951.

601. "Simba," Ebony, 11:73-76, Jan. 1956.

602. "Sins of Rachel Cade," Sepia, 9:50-53, Jan. 1961.

603. "Skirts Ahoy," Ebony, 7:44-46+, Apr. 1952.

604. "Solomon and Sheba," Ebony, 15:85-88, Feb. 1960.

605. "Something of Value," Ebony, 12:123-124+, Apr. 1957.

606. "Soul to Soul," Essence, 2:18, Nov. 1971.

607. "Sound and the Fury," Ebony, 14:127-128+, May 1959.

608. "South Pacific," Ebony, 13:76-79, June 1958.

609. "A Star is Born," Ebony, 10:91-92, Ja. 1955.

610. "Steel Helmet," Ebony, 6:78-80, Mar. 1951.

611. "The Story of a Three-day Pass," Ebony, 23:54-60, Sept. 1968.

612. "O'Neal defends Superfly," Daily Variety, 157:1, Sept. 14, 1972.

613. "Sweetback," Black World, 21:43-48, Nov. 1971.

614. "Sweetback," Ebony, 27:16-18+, Sept. 1971.

615. "Sweetback: the ego is willing but the aptitude is weak." Gary Arnold, Washington Post, May 30, 1971, p. E3.

616. "Tamango," Sepia, 8:24-27, Jan. 1960.

617. "Tarzan's Fight for Life," Ebony, 13:59-62, July 1958.

618. "Tarzan's perils," Our World, 6:9-10, Apr. 1951.

619. "Ten Commandments," Ebony, 12:59-60+, Nov. 1956.

620. "That Certain Feeling," Ebony, 11:75-76+, June 1956.

621. "To Kill a Mockingbird," Sepia, 12:32-33, May 1963.

622. "To Sir, with Love," Ebony, 22:68-70+, Apr. 1967.

623. "To Sir, with Love," Sepia, 16:76-79, Apr. 1967.

624. "Toxi," Ebony, 8:67-68+, January 1953.

625. "Trial," Ebony, 11:29-30+, Nov. 1955.

626. "Unchained," Ebony, 10:107-110, Nov. 1954.

627. "Unchained," Our World, 9:24-27, Nov. 1954.

628.   "Uptight: film starring a black anti-hero," Ebony, 24:
       46-8, Nov. 1968.

629.   "Vera Cruz," Our World, 10:36-37, March 1955.

630.   "The Well: false kidnapping is theme of thrilling film,"
       Our World, 6:58-59, Oct. 1951.

631.   "Whipped," Our World, 5:53, Mar. 1950.

632.   "White Witch Doctor," Our World, 8:8+, May 1953.

633.   "Within Our Gates," Chicago Defender, Jan. 10, 1920,
       p. 6.

634.   "Without Pity," Our World, 5:37, May 1950.

635.   "Wonderful Country," Ebony, 15:109-110+, Dec. 1959.

636.   "Young Man with a Horn," Ebony, 5:51-53, Dec. 1949.

637.   "Your Very Own; homeless children find new parents,
       new lives," Ebony, 14:113-114, May 1959.

BLACKS, FILMS, AND POLITICS

638.   "Negro actors hit 'Red front' meet," Hollywood Re-
       porter, June 13, 1952.

639.   "Negro actors tell stand on ASP parley," Los Angeles
       Examiner, June 13, 1952.

640.   "Red Slant," New York Times, May 20, 1951.
       (Concerning the "current attack by the Communist
       press on Hollywood's efforts to make enlightened
       and progressive films about the American Negro."
       Focal point: V. J. Jerome's The Negro in Holly-
       wood Films.)

641.   "Reds map Negro agitation: Commie-front ASP plans
       production and picketing; meeting attended by 500,"
       Hollywood Reporter, June 16, 1952.
       ("Production of films, picketing of studios and pub-
       lication of a new magazine described by John

Howard Lawson as an 'agitational' publication are among activities planned by the Arts, Sciences and Professions Council, named by federal and state authorities as a red front organization under the guise of obtaining more 'equality' for Negroes in the motion picture industry.... ")

642. "Top Negro actors rap ASPC meet here as 'Red promoted'," Los Angeles Daily News, June 13, 1952.
("Leading Negro actors ... repudiated a conference on equal rights for Negroes in the entertainment business scheduled ... by the Arts, Sciences and Professions Council. A statement was signed by Negro leaders in the AFL Screen Actors guild, asserting that the conference is being promoted in the official Communist press.... ")

BLACKS, FILMS, AND SOCIAL TENSIONS

643. "Black comedy any answer in the ghetto?" Patricia E. Davis, Los Angeles Herald Examiner, March 31, 1968, p. C11.

644. "Brando fights for civil rights," Ebony, 18:60-62+, Oct. 1963.

645. "Brando group denies 'rabble-rousing' cry," Los Angeles Times, Aug. 24, 1963.

646. "The Burning Cross: daring new Hollywood film exposes Ku Klux Klan," Ebony, 2:36-41, Sept. 1947.

647. "Can a 'laff riot' cure the other kind?" Patricia E. Davis, Los Angeles Times, Mar. 31, 1968.

648. "8 Atlanta nabes admitting Negroes," Variety Weekly, Aug. 7, 1963.

649. "Film stars aid Negroes," Hollywood Citizen-News, Aug. 23, 1963.
(Marlon Brando, Paul Newman, Anthony Franciosa and William Frye in Gadsden, Alabama.)

650. "Fla. theatres' racial policies still an issue," Variety

Weekly, Aug. 7, 1963.

651. "Four actors address Negro rally in Alabama, " Los
      Angeles Times, Aug. 23, 1963.

652. "Hollywood hitching no vehicles to current hot headlines
      of U. S. racial tensions, " Daily Variety, March 12,
      1965.

653. "Intruder in the Dust: film version of Faulkner novel
      is powerful anti-lynch document, " Ebony, 4:25-28,
      Aug. 1949.

654. "Jail threat; actors deny racial stir; Brando, et al.,
      in Alabama, " Los Angeles Herald Examiner, Aug. 23,
      1963.

655. "Lawless: famed B-picture producers spotlight lynch
      mob in new film on plight of United States Mexicans, "
      Ebony, 5:59-62, May 1950.

656. "Mayor in Alabama rebuffs four actors, " New York
      Times, Aug. 24, 1963.

657. "Pix gains 'disappoint' NAACP: taking hard look at new
      federal law, " A. D. Murphy, Daily Variety, July 23,
      1965.

658. "Q. T. Boycott of Negro films, " Variety Weekly,
      Mar. 25, 1959, p. 17.
           (On "unofficial" determination of Mississippi theatres
           to pass up any films dealing with racial or racist
           themes.)

659. "The Sound Track" [Column], William Mooring, The
      New York Tidings, June 2, 1944.
           (Some 500 screen and radio actors and writers in
           New York hope to enforce a three-point entertain-
           ment plan, ostensibly in the interests of social
           justice for the Negro.)

660. "South still snubs Negro films, " Variety Weekly, Apr.
      7, 1954, p. 5.

661. "Stars join drive against bigotry: Hollywood speaks up
      amid pressure by NAACP, " New York Times, July
      15, 1963.

662.   "Three Negroes convicted in N. C. trespass case, "
        <u>Motion Picture Exhibitor</u>, Jan. 22, 1964.

ALPHABETICAL PERIODICAL LISTINGS

AMERICA

"More about black films, " 127:459-60, Nov. 25, 1972.

"Negro actors in dramatic roles, " 115:298-300, Sept. 17, 1966.

AMERICAN FILM INSTITUTE

"The silent minority, " Stephen Zito, pp. 2-3, May 1971. (Early Black film companies and their productions.)

BLACK CREATION

"Clayton Riley on the Black critic, " 3:15, Summer 1972.

"The day Black movie stars got militant, " 4:40, Winter 1973.
(Black Artist Alliance for quality presentation and representation of Blacks in the movie industry.)

"Director Ossie Davis talks about Black girl, " 4:38-39, Winter 1973.

"Expanding world of the Black film" [editorial], 4:25, Winter 1973.

"Film as a tool for liberation?" 4:36-37, Winter 1973.

"A futuristic fable, " 4:43, Winter, 1973.

"History lesson: the boom is really an echo, " 4:32-34, Winter 1973.

"The independents: hard road for the old and new, "
3:8-11, Spring 1972.

"St. Clair Bourne: alternative Black visions, "   Michael
Mattox, 4:32-34, Summer 1973.
    (Article concerning Chamba Productions, Inc.)

"The subject is money, "   4:26, Winter 1973.
    (Lists Black directors, screenwriters, producers
    and scorers, academy award nominations since 1939.
    Current and recent Black film companies, Black
    distributors, Black films [studio count] from 1967-
    72.   Press coverage of the Black film "boom. ")

"The ten most important Black films between 1962 and
1972" [list], 4:2, Winter 1973.
    (Chosen for their "impact" on the Black community
    and the movie industry.)

"West coast gets the shaft, "   3:12-14, Summer 1972.

"William Greaves: creatively independent, " 4:10-11,
Fall 1972.

BLACK STARS

"The Black woman as a sex image in films, "   2:32-39,
Dec. 1972.

BLACK THEATRE

"Cotton comes to Harlem, "   5:47-49, 1971.

BLACK WORLD

"Sweet Sweetback's Baadasssss Song, "   21:43-48, Nov.
1971.

BOX OFFICE

"Black film festival now offered in Indianapolis, "   May
14, 1973.

THE BROWN AMERICAN

"The Negro theatre, "   1:16+, December 1936.

BUSINESS SCREEN

"A concerned filmmaker" [William Greaves], Sept. 1970.

CATHOLIC WORLD

"A modern miracle play--Green Pastures, "   Euphemia
V. R. Wyatt, 131:210-211, May 1930.

CHICAGO DEFENDER

"A report on filmland, "   Walter White, May 8, 1943.

"Within Our Gates" [latest Oscar Micheaux production],
Jan. 10, 1920, p. 6.

CHRISTIAN CENTURY

"Movies turn deaf ear to colored plea, "   47:1140,
Sept. 24, 1930.
    (Editorial on the unheeding of Black protest against
    The Birth of a Nation.)

"NCOMP charges Hollywood lacks Black sensitivity, "
86:1157, Sept. 10, 1969.

CINEMA

"Black American cinema: a primer, "   Norman Kagan,
6:2, Fall 1970.
    (A history of Black American filmmaking.)

CINEMEDITOR

"It could only happen in jolly Hollywood, "   pp. 8-18,
Fall 1970.

COLLIER'S

"Carmen Jones, "   113:14-15, Jan. 15, 1944.

COLOR

"Don Blackman's big role in Santiago, "   11:7-9, Aug.
1956.

COMMENTARY

"Two social scientists view No Way Out: the conscious
versus the 'message' in an anti-bias film, "   M. Wolfenstein, N. Leites,   10:388-391, Oct. 1950.

COMMONWEAL

"Black and white: the screen, "   Colin L. Westerbeck,
Jr. ,   96:285-6, May 26, 1972.
    (Critique of Black films Georgia, Georgia, Buck and
    the Preacher, Cool Breeze.)

"Black, white and technicolor, "   90:543-5, Sept. 5, 1969.
    ("Instead of just making films with some Negro
    actors, the studios would be wise to begin their
    planning with Negro culture, realistic Negro themes."
    Discussion of The Learning Tree and Sidney Poitier's
    films.)

"Era of dummies and darkies, "   Stephen Fay, 93:125-
8, Oct. 30, 1970.
    ("An argument could be made that the single ambi-
    tion of the screen darkie was to teach Shirley
    Temple to dance. ")

"Guess who's coming to lunch?"   Philip T. Hartung,
88:571, Aug. 23, 1968.
    (Integration in movies and the film industry.)

CORONET

"Negro and white love scenes that shock-it-to-you!"
Apr. 1969. pp. 10-17.

CRISIS

"Angelitos Negros, " 57:221-225+, Apr. 1950.

"The Birth of a Nation, " 14:25-26, May 1917.
(Concerning the protest of the film by Blacks in
Dayton, Ohio.)

"Go for Broke: a going Uncle Tom movie, " George
Yamada, 60:17-19, Jan. 1953.
(In article "Old Stereotyped pattern. ")

"Gordon Parks releases second movie (Shaft), " 78:162,
July 1971.

"Hollywood's new Negro films, " Loren Miller, 45:8,
Jan. 1938.

"Mulatto, " 57:698-699, Dec. 1950.

"Old stereotyped pattern, " George Yamada, 60:17-19,
Jan. 1953.

"Uncle Tom in Hollywood, " Loren Miller, 41:329,
Nov. 1934.
(Further protest against such films as The Birth of
a Nation.)

DAILY VARIETY

"After 'big scare' Hollywood using darkest Negroes
around, " Oct. 11, 1963, p. 1.

"All-American newsreel, " Mar. 7, 1945.

"Black pic cycle mushrooming, " Sept. 14, 1972, p. 1.

"Blaxploitation group vows fight vs. film industry, "
Sept. 14, 1972, p. 1.

"Definite increase in Hollywood jobs for Negro performers reported, " Aug. 21, 1963, p. 1.

"Goldwyn, Jr. , Negro feature series to star [Raymond]
St. Jacques, [Godfrey] Cambridge, and [Calvin] Lockhart. " Apr. 3, 1969, p. 1.

"Griffin bails out of Blaxploitation coalition post, "
Aug. 10, 1972, p. 3.

"Hollywood and the Negro musician, "   Henry Roth,
Feb. 17, 1964, p. 12.

"Hollywood hitching no vehicles to current hot headlines
of U. S. racial tensions, "   Mar. 12, 1965, p. 3.

"Many of 50 [Black films] planned may not materialize,
but 20 actually being planned, "   Aug. 14, 1972.

"More Italo pic parts for U. S. Negroes, "   June 7,
1968, p. 9.

"NAACP to mount drive in June for more jobs in pix, "
May 5, 1965, p. 2.

"Negro actors organization disputes Wilkins' view of
Hollywood, "   Dec. 9, 1964, p. 1.

"O'Neal defends Superfly, "   Sept. 14, 1972, p. 1.

"Pix gains 'disappoint' NAACP, "   A. D. Murphy, July
23, 1965, p. 1.

"Smith first Negro dialog coach, "   Apr. 9, 1968, p. 2.

"Theatrical, TV film industries pledge to depict Negroes 'as in real life', "   Oct. 28, 1957, p. 1.

"Thesps from racial minorities getting 8-9% of roles
in Hollywood pic and television, "   A. D. Murphy,
March 14, 1966, p. 1.

"Token use of Negroes in pix and television could be
dangerous, "   Dave Kaufman, Jan. 23, 1969, p. 1.

"[Vincent] Tubbs first Negro film council rep. , " July 5,
1963, p. 1.

"Valenti lauds Hyman for hiring Negro director, "   May
13, 1968, p. 1.

"Whitney Young urges Blacks set up their own production companies, "   Nov. 6, 1970, p. 3.

DAILY VARIETY (cont.)

>   "[Darryl] Zanuck pledges fair 20th shake in casting Ne-
>   groes, "   Oct. 4, 1962, p. 1.

DRAMA REVIEW

>   "Black movies/Black theatre, "   James P. Murray,
>   16:56-61, Dec. 1972.

EBONY

>   "Actor Satch: ageless hurler plays cavalry sergeant, "
>   15:109-110, Dec. 1959.
>   (Satchel Paige.)
>
>   "All the young men, "   Ebony, 15:83-84+, Aug. 1960.
>
>   "Althea's film debut, "   14:73-74, July 1959.
>   (Althea Gibson.)
>
>   "American in Italian movies, "   15:85-86+, June 1960.
>
>   "Anatomy of a Murder, "   14:106-108, Sept. 1959.
>
>   "Anatomy of a Murder: Hollywood uses talents of Duke
>   Ellington in movie, "   14:135-138, Sept. 1959.
>
>   "Androcles and the Lion, "   7:39-42+, Aug. 1952.
>
>   "Angelitos Negros, "   5:48-50, Feb. 1950.
>
>   "Anna Lucasta: Eartha Kitt, Sammy Davis star in
>   film, "   14:72-76, Dec. 1958.
>
>   "Anna's Sin, "   9:33-36, Mar. 1953.
>
>   "Any Number Can Play, "   4:24-26, May 1949.
>
>   "Balcony, "   12:64-65, Apr. 1963.
>
>   "Band of Angels, "   12:58-61, Sept. 1957.
>
>   "Battle among the beauties, "   29:144-45, Nov. 1973.

"Benny Goodman Story, " 11:77-80, Feb. 1956.

"Black cinema expo '72: Black cinema library-research center, " 27:151-4, May 1972.

"Black Gold, " 2:39, Oct. 1947.

"Black Like Me, " 19:37-38+, May 1964.

"The Black man as movie hero: new films offer a different male image, " Theophilus Green, 27:144-148, Aug. 1972.

"Blackboard Jungle, Sidney Poitier key role in brutal film about teacher, juvenile delinquents, " 10:87-88, May 1955.

"Body and Soul, " 2:16-17, Aug. 1947.

"Brando fights for civil rights, " 18:60-62+, Oct. 1963.

"Brock Peters, " 18:106-112, June 1963.

"The Burning Cross, " 2:36-41, Sept. 1947.

"Businessmen push fair job drive, " 6:15-18+, Aug. 1951.

"Canada Lee back in ring, " 2:16-17, Aug. 1947.

"The Cardinal, " 19:126-128+, Dec. 1963.

"Chicago slums are recreated in Buenos Aires for film scenes: Wright explains ideas about movie making, " 6:84-85, Jan. 1951.
    (Native Son.)

"A Child Waits, " 18:89-90+, Mar. 1963.

"China Gate, " 12:74+, June 1957.

"Cool World, " 20:43-44+, July 1965.

"Crooner Nat 'King' Cole turns actor, " 12:74 June 1957.

"Dandridge gets red carpet treatment, " 11:24, Aug. 1956.

EBONY (cont.)

"Decks Ran Red: in 8th movie, Dorothy Dandridge displays acting skill," 14:60-62, Nov. 1958.

"Deep is the Well," 6:38-42, Feb. 1951.

"Defiant Ones," 13:80-82+, Oct. 1958.

"Demetrius and the Gladiators," 9:91-94, Nov. 1953.

"Detective Story," 7:95-98, Dec. 1951.

"Diary of Anne Frank," 14:57-59, June 1959.

"Do Negroes have a future in Hollywood?" 11:24, Dec. 1955.

"Dorothy Dandridge's greatest triumph," 10:37-41, July 1955.

"Edge of the City," 12:75-76+, May 1957.

"The Egyptian," 9:83-86, Aug. 1954.

"The emancipation orgasm: Sweetback in wonderland," Lerone Bennet, Jr., 27:16-18+, Sept. 1971.

"Expanding world of Sidney Poitier," L. Robinson, 27:1-11+, Nov. 1971.

"Football heroes invade Hollywood," 24:195-7, Oct. 1969.
      (J. Brown, Woody Strode, O. J. Simpson.)

"French movie star: Moune de Rivel," 8:103-108, March 1953.

"From actor to college professor," 8:122-126, Nov. 1952.
      (Juano Hernandez.)

"From model to movie star," 26:128, June 1971.
      (Richard Roundtree.)

"Glory Alley," 7:100-102+, May 1952.

"Grace through exercise (Dorothy Dandridge). " 14:33-36, Mar. 1959.

"Guess Who's Coming to Dinner, " 23:56-58+, Jan. 1968.

"Harder They Fall: Joe Walcott is convincing actor in first movie role, " 11:87-90, May 1956.

"High Society, " 14:83-84+, Aug. 1959.

"High Society: new movie with jazz angle has role made for Satchmo, " 11:103-105, July 1956.

"Hole in the Head, " 14:83-84+, Aug. 1959.

"Hollywood debut for Pearl Bailey, " 2:38-39, Apr. 1947.

"Hollywood stunt girl, " 27:147-148+, Dec. 1971.
    (Peaches Jones.)

"Hollywood's first Negro movie star: Sidney Poitier breaks film barrier to become screen idol, " Lerone Bennett, Jr. , 14:100-103, May 1959.

"Home of the Brave, " 4:59-62, June 1949.

"Horse Soldiers, " 14:73-74+, July 1959.

"How movies are made, " 2:40-43, Mar. 1947.

"I came back from the dead, " 10:49-52, Mar. 1955.
    (Rex Ingram.)

"I didn't want to play a bigot, " 15:68-70+, Nov. 1959.
    (Robert Ryan.)

"Imitation of Life: Juanita Moore stars in new version of film, " 14:70-73, Apr. 1959.

"The Intruder, " 17:76-79, May 1962.

"Intruder in the Dust, " 4:25-28, Aug. 1948.

"Island in the Sun, " 12:32-34+, July 1957.

"Jackie Robinson Story, " 5:87-88+, June 1950.

EBONY (cont.)

"James Earl Jones: actor still climbing, "   20:98-106,
Apr. 1965.

"Jedda, "   12:108+, March 1957.

"King, from Montgomery to Memphis, "   25:172-174,
Apr. 1970.

"Knock on Any Door, "   4:34-38, Jan. 1949.

"Last Angry Man, "   15:42-44, Jan. 1960.

"Lawless, "   5:59-62, May 1950.

"Lena Horne enjoys her longest vacation, "   10:64-68,
Dec. 1954.

"Lena Horne speaks freely: on race, marriage, stage, "
Robert Feinstein, 18:61-67, May 1963.

"Let No Man Write My Epitaph, "   15:94-96+, Oct. 1960.

"Lights Out, "   6:87-88+, Dec. 1950.

"Lilies of the Field, "   18:55-58, Oct. 1963.

"Lost Boundaries, "   4:51-53, July 1949.

"Lydia Bailey, "   7:39-44, Jan. 1952.

"Madi Comfort: newest movie queen, "   10:25-28, Sept.
1955.

"Mambo, "   10:83-84+, Dec. 1954.

"Man and Boy, "   L. Robinson, 26:42-44, Apr. 1971.

"Member of the Wedding, "   8:47-51, Dec. 1952.
       (Ethel Waters.)

"Miss Waters regrets, "   12:56-60, Feb. 1957.

"Moby Dick: calypso singer Edric Connor plays choice
role in adventurous film about whaling men, "   10:107-
109, Sept. 1955.

"Moby Dick, "   10:107-109, Sept. 1955.

"Movie choir, "   4:25-27, Oct. 1949.
      (Jester Hairston Choir.)

"Movie debut, "   4:25, Apr. 1949.
      (James Edwards.)

"Movie features blossoming star, "   13:93-94, Nov. 1957,
      (Tommie Moore in Green-eyed Blond for Warner
      Brothers.)

"Movie maker Belafonte, "   14:94-96, July 1959.

"Movie musicals; ranking Negro performers given
musical bits in half-dozen coming Hollywood production,"
6:51-53, Aug. 1951.

"Movie starlet's Roman holiday, "   10:27-30+, Jan. 1950.
      (Tessa Prendergast.)

"Naked Maja, "   14:103-105, Feb. 1959.

"Native Son filmed in Argentina, "   6:82-86, Jan. 1951.

"New bad guy of the movies, "   22:171-172+, June 1967.
      (Raymond St. Jacques.)

"New films: culture or con game?"   28:60-2, Dec. 1972.

"No Way Out, "   5:31-34, Mar. 1950.

"None But the Brave, "   19:110-112+, Oct. 1964.

"Nothing But a Man, "   20:198-201, Apr. 1965.

"Odds Against Tomorrow, "   15:68-70+, Nov. 1959.

"Of Men and Music, 6:49-50+, May 1951.
      (Marian Anderson.)

"100 years of Negro entertainment, "   Allen Morrison,
18:122-4, Sept. 1963.

"Our Man in Havana, "   15:66+, March 1960.

"Paris Blues, "   16:46-50, Aug. 1961.

EBONY (cont.)

"The Peanut Man, " 2:48-50, July 1947.

"Pete Kelley's Blues, Ella Fitzgerald draws a hot jazz assignment for her first major role in movies, " 10: 115-117, Oct. 1955.

"Pinky, " 4:23-25, Sept. 1949.

"Pool of London, " 6:59-61, Oct. 1951.

"A pooped Pearlie Mae, " 13:55-56, Apr. 1958.

"President's Lady: Vera Francis gets explosive role in movie touching on mixed romantic theme, " 8:71-75, Feb. 1953.

"Pressure Point, " 18:45-46+, Nov. 1962.

"Prisoner of War, " 9:77-80+, June 1954.

"Private world of Dorothy Dandridge, " 17:116-121, June 1962.

"Raisin in the Sun, " 16:53-56+, Apr. 1961.

"Raymond the magnificent, " Charles Sanders, 25:175-178+, Nov. 1969.
        (Raymond St. Jacques.)

"Red Ball Express, " 7:51-54, June 1952.

"Robin and the Seven Hoods, " 19:90-92+, June 1964.

"Sailor to movie star, " 8:46-51, Aug. 1953.
        (Danny Williams.)

"St. Louis Blues, Nat 'King' Cole plays lead role in film biography of W. C. Handy, " 13:27-28, May 1958.

"Sapphire, " 15:51-54+, Dec. 1959.

"Screen test; Dorothy Dandridge wins Carmen Jones title role with sizzling performance, " 9:37-40, Sept. 1954.

"Secret of a movie maid, " 5:52-56+, Nov. 1949.

"Sergeant Rutledge, " 15:75-76+, July 1960.

"Showboat: William Warfield makes film debut in re-vival, " 6:69-71, Jan. 1951.

"Sidney Poitier: the man behind the star, " Charles Sanders, 23:172-174+, Apr. 1968.

"Simba, " 11:73-76, Jan. 1956.

"Skirts Ahoy, " 7:44-46+, Apr. 1952.

"Solomon and Sheba, " 15:85-88, Feb. 1960.

"Something of Value, " 12:123-124+, Apr. 1957.

"Sound and the Fury, " 14:127-128+, May 1959.

"South Pacific, " 13:76-79, June 1958.

"Sportin' life and the strange 'lady', " 14:99-98, Feb. 1959.

"A Star is Born, " 10:91-92+, Jan. 1955.

"Star of Italian movies: John Kitzmiller, " 7:71-73, Nov. 1951.

"Steel Helmet, " 6:78-80, Mar. 1951.

"Stepin Fetchit comes back, " 7:64-67, Feb. 1952.

"The Story of a Three-day Pass: French film pushes Melvin Van Peebles into ranking of award winning di-rectors, " 23:54-60, Sept. 1968.

"Take a Giant Step: Singer Johnny Nash makes debut as actor, " 14:48-51, Sept. 1959.

"Tarzan's Fight for Life, " 13:59-62, July 1958.

"Teenagers win movie roles, " 18:150-152, May 1963.
    (Judy Pace and two other interracial starlets.)

"Ten Commandments: over 100 Negro extras work in

EBONY (cont.)

DeMille Bible spectacle.   12:59-60+, Nov. 1956.

"That Certain Feeling, "   11:75-76+, June 1956.

"To Sir, with Love, "   22:68-70+, Apr. 1967.

"Tony Curtis photographs Sergeants Three, "   17:43-44+, Apr, 1962.

"Toxi, "   8:67-68+, Jan. 1953.

"Trial, "   11:29-30+, Nov. 1955.

"Trina Parks: the girl who zaps James Bond, "   27:68-70, Mar. 1972.
   (In Diamonds Are Forever)

"Unchained, "   10:107-110, Nov. 1954.

"Uptight: film starring a black anti-hero, "   24:46-48, Nov. 1968.

"Why I played a film bigot, "   Bobby Darin, 18:46-46+, Nov. 1962.

"Why I played Jim, the slave, "   Archie Moore, 15:43-44+, Sept. 1960.

"Why Negroes don't like Eartha Kitt, "   10:29-38, Dec. 1954.

"Why Negroes don't like Porgy and Bess, "   B. Thompson, 14:50-52, Oct. 1952.

"Why the stars go broke, "   18:84-88, July 1963.
   (The cases of Dorothy Dandridge, Stepin Fetchit, Ethel Waters, and some sports stars.)

"Wonderful Country, "   15:109-110+, Dec. 1959.

"Yank movie man of Japan, "   18:45-46+, July 1963.
   (Arthur "Chico" Lourant.)

"Young Man with a Horn, "   5:51-53, Dec. 1949.

"Your Very Own: homeless children find new parents, new lives, " 14:113-114, May 1959.

ENCORE

"Otto Preminger on Black movies, " 2:56-59, Aug. 1973.

"Which way the Black film?" 2:52-54, Jan. 1973.

ENTERTAINMENT WORLD

"Hollywood: in glorious Black and white, " Leonard Feather, Dec. 12, 1969.

ESSENCE

"Ain't 'Beulah' dead yet? or images of the Black woman in film" 4:61+, May 1973.

"A bad Black image in film, " 4:70, May 1973.

"Black imagery on the silver screen, " 3:34, Dec. 1972. (Evolution in Black films from Shaft to Sounder.)

"Buck and the Preacher, " 3:8, Aug. 1972.

"A flood of Black films, " 5:28, Sept. 1972. (Whereas a few years ago there was scarcely a Black film, nowadays there are more and more because of the Black film "fad, " which will yield to a growth of better films.)

"Gordon Parks, " 3:62+, Oct. 1972.

"Paul Winfield: a man unto himself, " 4:27, June 1973.

"Shaft, " 2:76, Aug. 1971.

"Soul to soul, " 2:18, Nov. 1971.

ETUDE

"Worthwhile music in the movies: much choral work

ETUDE (cont.)

> done by Negro organization, " Verna Arvey, 57:152,
> Mar. 1939.
>> (Negro choral groups working on movies in Holly-
>> wood.)

FILM CULTURE

> "Tribute to Paul Robeson, " Fall, Winter 1970.

FILM DAILY

> "Burt Lancaster sees Negro advance in films, " March
> 1, 1968.

> "Negroes still given racially oriented pic roles: O.
> Davis, " Allen C. Lobsenz, Oct. 1, 1965.

FILM QUARTERLY

> "Beige, brown or black, " Albert Johnson, 13:38-43,
> Fall, 1959.
>> (Analysis of filmdom's approach to interracialism,
>> which is characterized as "vague, inconclusive, and
>> undiscussed. ")

> "The Negro in American films: some recent works, "
> Albert Johnson, 18:14-30, Summer 1965.
>> (Analysis of efforts to portray the "Black Problem"
>> in several movies of the 60's, including several
>> Poitier films.)

> "Stepin' Fetchit talks back; interview, " 24:20-26, Sum-
> mer 1971.

FILM-TV DAILY

> "'Black America' focus on Hollywood influence, " June
> 25, 1968.

> "No color line in casting: [Jim] Brown and Raquel
> Welch, " Mar. 24, 1968.

"Non-acting film, video jobs for Blacks up 48% in
1969, " Vance King, March 12, 1970.

FILMS AND FILMING

"How Hollywood is smashing the colour bar, " Sidney
Harmon, 5:7+, Mar. 1959.
(The author contends that "films are now breaking
the chains of racial prejudice, " using Anna Lucasta
as a case in point.)

"The Negro in cinema, " Earl Cameron, 3:9-11, May
1957.
(How the color bar in the studios is being broken.)

FILMS IN REVIEW

"The Negro in films today, " Arthur Knight, Feb. 1950,
pp. 14-19.

FREEDOMWAYS

"The Negro in American films, " Carlton Moss, 3:134-
142, Spring 1963.

HISTORIAN

"Reaction of the Negro to the motion picture Birth of a
Nation, " Thomas Cripps, 25:344-362, May 1963.

HOLLYWOOD CITIZEN-NEWS

"Film stars aid Negroes, " Aug. 23, 1963.

"Hollywood lauded on Negro hiring, " Dec. 2, 1964.

"Movie boycott threat, " Oct. 9, 1969.

"NCI director says report lied, only 1 Black trainee
hired, " Oct. 14, 1969.

"Negro critics form group, " Nov. 19, 1949.

HOLLYWOOD CITIZEN-NEWS (cont.)

"Negro film roles show sharp increase," Apr. 22, 1969.

"Writer says Blacks need own film heroes," May 15, 1970.
(Joe Greene, creator of "Superspade.")

HOLLYWOOD REPORTER

"Black backers set hard line: big demand for film dollar," Ron Pennington, Nov. 7, 1973, p. 3.

"Black capitalism big factor in PUSH drive on Hollywood," Will Tusher, Aug. 18, 1970.

"Black producers mass to generate financing," Will Tusher, June 29, 1973, p. 1.

"Black vise tightens; demand censorship on Black pictures," Will Tusher, Sept. 20, 1972.

"Brown outlines Black union plans 'self-determination'," Collette Wood, Aug. 26, 1969.

"Central hires Negro," July 13, 1967.

"Color bar dissolves on selling, Negro actors find," Bob Hull, May 6, 1968.

"Gordon Parks tells of union aid on Learning," Aug. 14, 1969.

"Lou Rawls stars in first all-Black cowboy movie," Collette Wood, Sept. 17, 1969.

"Negro actors hit 'Red front' meet," June 13, 1952.

"Negro actors should act, not be diverted, says Yaphet Kotto," June 4, 1968.

"New producing unit for Negro talent," Oct. 3, 1955.

"Peters forms Black production company, sets initial projects," Mar. 20, 1973.

(Thomas Peters, founder of Indepth Productions.)

"Producers suggest Negro job center," Apr. 21, 1967.

"Raymond St. Jacques claims critics pamper Black films," Ron Pennington, Jan. 8, 1973, p. 13.

"Reds map Negro agitation," June 16, 1952.

"Studio films schedules 12 Negro featurettes," Jan. 12, 1955.

"This may be year industry makes itself clear as far as Negro is concerned, says Brock Peters," Feb. 12, 1968.

JET

"The Cry of Jazz," Negro produced and directed documentary film depicting through jazz the Negro's struggle...," p. 62, Feb. 18, 1960.

"Great White Hope," 39:58, Feb. 25, 1971.

"Public finally to see documentary on Angela Davis," 41:47, Nov. 25, 1971.

"Sidney Poitier makes relevant film for Blacks," C. S. Thompson, 41:58-61, May 13, 1971.

"Strode is brilliant as 'Black Jesus'," 41:53, Oct. 7, 1971.

"U. S. Equal Employment Opportunity Commission calls for job bias suit against giant movie makers," 35:58-59, Apr. 3, 1969.

JOURNAL OF NEGRO EDUCATION

"The American Negro: an annotated list of educational films and film-strips," 33:79-82, Winter 1964.

JOURNAL OF RELIGIOUS THOUGHT

"Secular prophecy in an age of film," 27:63-75, Spring-

JOURNAL OF RELIGIOUS THOUGHT (cont.)

Summer 1970.

JOURNAL OF THE PRODUCER'S GUILD

"Actors and other minority groups," Charlton Heston,
10:35-37, Mar. 1968.

LIBERATION

"He who must die," 4:17-18, Mar. 1959.

LIBERATOR

"The Black boom," 4:16+, Aug. 1964.
(Comments on films Black Like Me and The Cool
World.)

LIFE

"Black Hollywood," Jan. 23, 1970, pp. M19-M21.

"Films for blacks: a new kind of exploitation flick,"
Richard Schickel, 72:20, Jun. 9, 1972.
(Review of Buck and the Preacher, Nigger Charley,
Soul Soldier, and Cool Breeze.)

"Real anger was backstage; racial tensions during
shooting of Halls of Anger," 69:2, Aug. 21, 1970.

LITERARY DIGEST

"Primitive emotions aflame in a Negro film," 103:42-
56, Oct. 5, 1929.
(Concerning a "talkie" dealing with the emotional
aspects of Southern Negroes.)

LOOK

"Poitier meets Belafonte," George Goodman, 35:56-

60, Aug. 24, 1971.
(Review of Buck and the Preacher.)

LOS ANGELES DAILY NEWS

"Top Negro actors rap ASPC meet here as 'Red promoted'," June 13, 1952.

LOS ANGELES EXAMINER

"Negro actors tell stand on ASP meeting," June 13,
1952.

LOS ANGELES HERALD EXAMINER

"Black comedy any answer in the ghetto?" Patricia E.
Davis, March 31, 1968, p. C11.

"The honest movies about Negroes--when?" Renata
Adler, Mar. 3, 1968.

"Jail threat," Aug. 23, 1963.

LOS ANGELES SENTINEL

"Celebrity marriages," Gertrude Gipson, Sept. 20,
1973, p. A1.

"Hell up in Harlem stars Fred Williamson," Oct. 11,
1973, p. B7.

"Jesse Jackson applauds Save the Children," Oct. 25,
1973, p. B9.

"Karate champion Jim Kelly makes movie debut," Sept.
6, 1973, p. B2A.

"Lady Sings the Blues," Oct. 4, 1973, p. B1A.
(Diana Ross.)

"Maurie," Sept. 6, 1973, p. B1A.
(Bernie Casey.)

LOS ANGELES SENTINEL (cont.)

"Negroes 'written out' of Hollywood movies," May 9,
1946, p. 12.
(Rather than present a true picture of the Negro in
its movies, Hollywood prefers to "write Negroes
out" of its scripts.)

"Pam Grier is Foxy Brown," Oct. 11, 1973, p. B6.

LOS ANGELES TIMES

"Ancient film's effect on modern Negro life," Roy
Wilkins, Feb. 15, 1965.
(The Birth of a Nation.)

"Another kind of Negro stereotype," Hal Humphrey,
Apr. 13, 1967, Part 5, p. 20.

"Award goes to Negro for movie work," Apr. 19, 1965.

"Brando group denies 'rabble-raising' cry," Aug. 24,
1963.

"Can a 'laff riot' cure the other kind," Patricia E.
Davis, Mar. 31, 1968.

"Don Williams," Mary Murphy, March 24, 1973.

"Film executive blames hiring bias on unions," Robert
Kistler, Oct. 19, 1969.

"Four actors address Negro rally in Alabama," Aug.
23, 1963.

"Hollywood gives more work roles to Negro," Harry
Bernstein, March 13, 1966, p. A2.

"I wish mom could see me now," Skip Ferderber, Nov.
22, 1973, pt. 4, p. 36.
(Matthew "Stymie" Beard, Jr.)

"Negro employment increases in films," Gene Handsaker, Sept. 11, 1967.

"Re-evaluation needed in film industry," Charles

Champlin, Apr. 9, 1968, pt. 4, p. 1.

"Take two of a movie miracle, " Art Seidenbaum, Jan. 6, 1968, pt. 3, p. 1.

"U. S. plans to prod film industry on job discrimination charge, " Vincent T. Burke, Oct. 19, 1969.

LOS ANGELES TIMES CALENDAR

"An assessment of the status of Hollywood Blacks, " Dan Knapp, Sept. 28, 1969.

"Hollywood's Negroes mired in stereotypes, " Burt Prelutsky, Feb. 19, 1967, p. 9.

"Makers of Black films stand at crossroads, " Jan. 28, 1973, p. 18.

MASSACHUSETTS REVIEW

"Paul Robeson and Black identity in American movies, " 11:468-85, Summer 1970.

MOTION PICTURE EXHIBITOR

"Three Negroes convicted in N. C. trespass case, " Jan. 22, 1964.

MOTION PICTURE HERALD

"Distributor lists Negro pictures, " Aug. 15, 1936.

"Goldberg plans 12 Negro features, " Apr. 14, 1945.

"Negroes movie-conscious; support 430 film houses, " Jan. 24, 1942, pp. 33-34.

"Race talks in Hollywood, " Aug. 7, 1963.

"232 Negro theatres 1-1/2% of all houses, " Apr. 24, 1937.

MOVIE/TV MARKETING

"Guess who's coming to cinema?" Edward Mapp, 24:
44, March 1970.

NATIONAL REVIEW

"Superspade's revenge, " 5:39-40, May 12, 1972.

NEGRO DIGEST

"Actors show how" [editorial], 2:63-64, Apr. 1944.
(Absence of discrimination in the union, Actors
Equity Association.)

"Blackface, Hollywood style, " Dalton Trumbo, 2:37-39,
Feb. 1944.

"'De Lawd' cooks with gas, " 2:53-54, Jan. 1944.
(Rex Ingram.)

"Do you remember 'Our Gang'?" 9:69-70, Dec. 1950.

"He passed as a Negro, " Al Weisman, 9:16-20, Oct.
1951.

"A Hollywood actress looks at the Negro, " Marsha
Hunt, 5:14-17, Sept. 1947.

"Hollywood and the Negro, " Robert G. Hunter, 15:37-
41, May 1966.

"Hollywood director speaks out, " Robert Ellis, 9:42-
44, Jan. 1951.
(Jewish director Mark Robson talks about race in
movies.)

"Hollywood's new deal for Negroes, " John T. McManus
and Louis Kronenberger, 4:77-80, June 1946.

"How Hollywood can better race relations, " John Garfield, 6:4-8, Nov. 1947.

"How Hollywood feels about Negroes, " Robert Jones,
5:4-8, Aug. 1947.

"Ida Lupino brings new hope to Hollywood, "   Robert
Ellis, 8:47-49, Aug. 1950.

"Is Hollywood fair to Negroes in its films?"   [Poll],
1:15-21, Apr. 1943.

"Khartoum, "   16:32-36₊, Feb. 1967.

"Movie star who hates his job, "   Robert Ellis, 9:81-83,
Dec. 1950.
      (Richard Widmark.)

"Movies in the ghetto B. P. [Before Poitier], "   18:21-
27, Fall 1969.

"Needed: A Negro film movement, "   Walter Moore,
15:45-48, Jan. 1966.

"The Negro and the movies, "   William Harvison, 2:19-
21, Aug. 1940.
      (Criticism of Negro portrayals and pictures.)

"Negro in the American theater, "   11:52-58, July 1962.

"Negro lobby in Hollywood, "   David O. Selznick, 4:27-
28, Aug. 1946.

"Nothing But a Man, "   14:49, May 1965.

"Peck on prejudice, "   Anne Strick, 6:17-20, July 1948.

"Problems facing Negro actors, "   Woodie King, Jr. ,
15:53-59, Apr. 1966.

"Race tolerance: newest box office hit, "   Peggy Weil,
6:46-49, Aug. 1948.

"Screen stereotypes, "   Leon H. Hardwick, 4:57-58,
May 1946.

"She passed for Negro--in the movies, "   8:26-27, Mar.
1950.
      (Jeanne Crain.)

"Stardom 'for Negroes only', "   Don Deleihbur, 3:87-88,
Nov. 1944.
      (Discrimination against mulattoes in show business.)

NEGRO DIGEST (cont.)

"The tattered queens, "   Ruby Dee,   15:32-36, Apr. 1966.

"Tooting Lena's Horn, "   Charlotte Kay, 3:25-29, Aug.
1945.

"Why I became an actor, "   11:80-97, Dec. 1961.
    (Sidney Poitier.)

"Young actor on the way up: James Earl Jones, "
Robert Burg, 15:26-31, Apr. 1966.

NEGRO HISTORY BULLETIN

"Dark horse operas: a film article, "   36:13-14, Jan.
1973.
    (Black westerns in the 30's.)

"Enroute to the future, "   30:30, Apr. 1967.

"Hollywood phony on Negro films, writer charges, "
24:21, Oct. 1960.

"The image makers, "   Edward Mapp, 26:127-128, Dec.
1962.

"Not by protest alone!"   31:12-14, Apr. 1968.
    (Young Black playwrights must make the Black
    characters plausible so that Blacks may get roles
    in films and on stage.)

"Passing years, "   22:93-94, Jan. 1959.
    (The Black man must write his own history of
    Blacks; but knowledge is lacking.)

"Return of the Emperor Jones, "   34:160-162, Nov. 1971.
    (Redistribution of Emperor Jones, starring Paul
    Robeson, after 25 years.)

NEW MASSES

"G'wan with the wind, "   James Dugan, 34:28, Jan. 2,
1940.

NEW REPUBLIC

"Birth of a Nation, " Francis Hackett, 2:185, Mar. 20,
1915.

"Stanley Kaufmann on films, " 168:20₊, Apr. 28, 1973.
(Comparison of the film The Mack with other Black
films.)

NEW YORK TIDINGS

"The sound track" [column], William Mooring, June 2,
1944.

NEW YORK TIMES

"About Negro directors, " Dec. 24, 1967.

"Belafonte: 'Look, ' they tell me, 'don't rock the boat', "
Harry Belafonte, Apr. 21, 1968.

"History of a dream, " W. E. B. Du Bois, Sept. 24,
1944.

"Hollywood acts on race problem, " Sept. 21, 1963,
p. 81.

"Hollywood change: Negroes gain in a new movie and
elsewhere, " Larry Glen, Sept. 22, 1963.

"Hollywood's boy and girl next door--color them white,"
Lindsay Patterson, June 16, 1968, p. D9.

"Is it better to be Shaft than Uncle Tom?" Aug. 26,
1973, p. D11.

"Mayor in Alabama rebuffs four actors, " Aug. 24, 1963.

"The Negro in films, " Bosley Crowther, Oct. 6, 1963.

"The Negro in films: Poitier points a dilemma which
The Cool World helps rebut, " Apr. 26, 1964.

"Red slant, " May 20, 1951.

NEW YORK TIMES (cont.)

"So now I'm back and Black and available, " Peter De
Anda, Oct. 10, 1971.

"Stars join drive against bigotry, " July 15, 1963.

"The still invisible man, " Peter Bart, July 17, 1966.

"To make the Negro a living human being, " Lindsay
Patterson, Feb. 18, 1968, p. 80.

"Why does white America love Sidney Poitier so?"
Clifford Mason, Sept. 10, 1967, p. 1.

NEW YORK TIMES MAGAZINE

"The Negro actor asks himself: am I a Negro or am I
an actor?" Walter Kerr, p. 34-35, Oct. 15, 1967.
("The Negro actor today is torn between an actor's
desire to 'impersonate anyone' and jobs employing
his uniqueness as a Negro'. ")

NEW YORKER

"Black film: God's step children, " 46:34-35, Apr. 18,
1970.

"Notes on black movies, " 48:159-165, Dec. 2, 1972.

NEWSWEEK

"Black movie boom, " 78:66, Sept. 6, 1971.

"Black movies: renaissance or rip off?" 80:74-78,
Oct. 23, 1972.

"Blacks vs. Shaft, " 80:88, Aug. 28, 1972.

NORFOLK JOURNAL AND GUIDE

"MGM creates a Black star: first in 60 years, " Apr.
10, 1971, p. 14.

(Richard Roundtree.)

OPPORTUNITY

"End of a controversy" [editorial], 13:231, Aug. 1935.
(Comments on Sterling A. Brown's critique of Imitation of Life.)

"Hearts in Dixie, " Robert Benchley, 7:122-123, Apr.
1929.

"Hollywood presents us: the movies and racial attitudes, " Cecil D. Halliburton, 13:296-297, Oct. 1935.
(Motion pictures continue to give negative portrayals
of the Black man.)

"They made good in the movie capital, " William Smallwood, 19:76-77, Mar. 1941.
(Hazel Washington and Mildred Blount, employees
in Hollywood.)

OUR WORLD

"ABC's of movieland, " Gertrude Gipson, 7:60-64, Sept.
1952.

"Aftermath: here is Marva ..., " 8:12-13, July 1953.
(The choosing of Hilda Simms to play the role of
Marva Louis in The Joe Louis Story.)

"Barbara's gal Friday, " 9:73, Aug. 1954.

"Bill Marshall: matinee idol, " 9:38-41, Feb. 1954.

"Black Samson, " 9:10, Mar. 1954.

"The Breaking Point, " 5:51, Aug. 1950.
(With Juano Hernandez.)

"Can Dandridge outshine Lena Horne?" 7:29-32, June
1952.

"Cruisin' Down the River, " 8:32-33, June 1953.

"Cry the Beloved Country: visiting actors taste South

OUR WORLD (cont.)

Africa's race hate while making movie, " 6:34-36, July 1951.

"The Gladiators, " 8:8+, Oct. 1953.

"Globe Trotters, " 5:36-38, June 1950.

"Hollywood: so what!" James Edwards, 8:56-59, Dec. 1953.

"Jackie Robinson Story, " 5:36-38, June 1950.

"Jamaica Sea, " 7:60-61, Dec. 1952.
    (with Bill Walker.)

"Lena Horne: Our World's first cover girl, " 5:11-13, Apr. 1950.

"Lydia Bailey, " 6:12-14, Dec. 1951.

"Lydia Bailey, " 7:46-53, Aug. 1952.

"Mme Sul-Te-Wan: at 80 she's the oldest Negro actress in Hollywood, " 9:80-82, Feb. 1954.

"Member of the Wedding, " 7:59-61, Oct. 1952.

"Moby Dick, " 10:62-64, June 1955.

"Moulin Rouge, " 8:8+, Mar. 1953.

"Mulatto, " 6:50, Jan. 1951.

"Native Son, " 5:36-38, Dec. 1950.

"No Way Out, " 5:32-33, Apr. 1950.

"Panic in the Streets, " 5:47, Nov. 1950.

"The passing of Beulah, " 8:12-15, Feb. 1953.

"Pool of London, " 6:43-45, Sept. 1951.

"Red Ball Express, " 7:42-43, Apr. 1952.

"See How They Run, " 7:10+, Nov. 1952.

"Strange love story: Negro movie company with ...
story on color prejudice among Negroes themselves, "
9:26-28, Mar. 1954.

"Tarzan's perils, " 6:9-10, Apr. 1951.

"Unchained, " 9:24-27, Nov. 1954.

"Vera Cruz, " 10:36-37, Mar. 1955.

"Vera Francis, movie's new sex thrill, " 8:56, Mar.
1953.

"The Well: false kidnapping is theme of thrilling film,"
6:58-59, Oct. 1951.
    (Stars Maidie Norman, Ernest Anderson, Gwendolyn
    Laster.)

"What's cookin' in Hollywood?" 7:62-63, Oct. 1952.
    (Favorite recipes of six Black actors, including
    Maidie Norman.)

"Whipped, " 5:53, Mar. 1950.

"White Witch Doctor, " 8:8+, May 1953.

"Without Pity, " 5:37, May 1950.

PHYLON

"Death of Rastus: Negroes in American films since
1945, " 28:267-275, Fall 1967.

"The Green Pastures again, " Doris B. Garey, 20:193-
194, Summer 1959.

"Hollywood report, " 6:13-16, Winter 1945.
    (Unchanging attitude of whites towards Blacks.)

"How genuine is The Green Pastures?" Nick Aaron
Ford, 20:67-70, Spring 1959.

"Prejudicial film: progress and stalemate, 1915-1967."
Anne K. Nelsen and Hart M. Nelsen, 31:142-147, Summer 1970.

PHYLON (cont.)

"Pro-Negro films in Atlanta, " [reprint], Gerald Weales, 13:298-304, Dec. 1952.
(Analysis of reactions to such films as Pinky, Home of the Brave.)

"The problem of Negro character and dramatic incident, " William Couch, Jr. , 11:127-133, June 1950.

PITTSBURGH COURIER

"Talented Alex Clarke is a bold Black actor, " Jan. 10, 1970, p. 12.

POLITICAL SCIENCE QUARTERLY

"Gamut from A to B: the image of the Black in pre-1915 movies, " D. J. Leab, 88:53-70, Mar. 1973.

QUARTERLY OF FILM, RADIO, AND TELEVISION

"The film gains a new dimension, " Jack Howard, 7:77, Fall 1952.

QUICK NEWS WEEKLY

"The Negro in entertainment, " Aug. 13, 1951.

READER'S DIGEST

"Three lives of Ethel Waters, " 101:81-85, Dec. 1972.

SATURDAY REVIEW

"The problem, " Hollis Alpert, 50:50, Jan. 21, 1967.

SATURDAY REVIEW OF THE ARTS

"First black movie stars; excerpt from Toms, Coons,

Mulattoes, Mammies and Bucks, " 1:24-29, Feb. 1973.

SENIOR SCHOLASTIC

"Black films: values, pro and con, " 101:8-9, Dec. 11, 1972.

SEPIA

"All the Young Men, " 8:56-61, June 1960.

"Allison Mills, " Walter Jenkins, 19:14-17, July 1970.

"Anna's Sin, " 10:38-40, May 1961.

"Athlete Rafer Johnson becomes top Hollywood star, " 11:58-62, June 1962.

"Barbara McNair, " 13:74-78, Apr. 1964.

"Beauty that is Barbara McNair, " 19:73-77, Nov. 1970.

"The Black girl who plays the wife of James Bond, " 11:35-42, May 1973.
    (Gloria Hendry.)

"Black Klansman, " 15:64-67, June 1966.

"The Black path to Hollywood, " 19:50-52+, Apr. 1970.
    (Gordon Parks.)

"Black playboy of Hollywood, " 20:64-68+, July 1971.
    (Raymond St. Jacques.)

"Crowning Experience, " A. D. Valle, 9:20-22, Feb. 1961.

"Diahann Carroll: talented bombshell, " 11:57-59, Mar. 1962.

"Do Black actors make good fathers?" 18:32-34, Dec. 1969.

"Fighting U. S. 10th Cavalry, " 16:52-57, Oct. 1967.
    (Company of horsemen organized to bring the ex-

SEPIA (cont.)

> ploits of the original 10th Cavalry of Black troops
> to the screen.)

"First African movie made by and about Africans, "
(Kongi's Harvest), John Bennett.   20:59-63, Sept.
1971.

"The girl who went nude for stardom, "   R. Clark, 20:
53-56, Oct. 1971.
> (French actress: Sylvette Cabrisseau.)

"Great athlete finds Hollywood stardom, " A. S. Young,
8:64-67, Aug. 1960.
> (Woody Strode.)

"Guns at Batasi, "   13:16-19, Nov. 1964.

"Harry Belafonte's debut as a Hollywood producer, "
A. S. Young, 7:34-39, July 1959.

"Hollywood hires a Negro director, "   12:35-38, Apr.
1963.
> (Wendell Franklin, assistant director of movie
> Greatest Story Ever Told.)

"Hollywood's busiest starlet, " A. S. Young, 7:40-45,
May 1959.
> (Dawn Finney, actress-singer-model.)

"Hollywood's most versatile starlet, " A. S. Young,
6:42-46, Dec. 1958.

"Hollywood's new Black beauties, "   22:37-44, Mar. 1973.

"Hollywood's new breed, "   12:20-25, June 1963.

"How liberal is show business, "   12:40-43, Mar. 1963.

"How Sidney Poitier won an Oscar, "   13:14-17, June '64.

"Is Hollywood afraid to star a sexy black actress?" 18:
10-15, June 1969.

"Ivan Dixon at home, "   16:38-41, Feb. 1967.

"James Earl Jones' goal is to become a great actor, "
13:72-76, Feb. 1964.

"James Earl Jones: race is still the important thing, "
20:16-17, Jan. 1971.

"Janet Maclachlan grabs filmland's brass ring, " 19:54-
58, Mar. 1970.

"Jim Brown, Rio Conchos, " 13:22-25, Dec. 1964.

"Kings Go Forth, " 6:65-69, May 1958.

"Life and death of Dorothy Dandridge, " A. S. Young,
14:8-12+, Dec. 1965.

"Living Between Two Worlds, " 13:62-66, Feb. 1964.
    (Writer-producer Horace Jackson's story of a young
    man torn between a career as a jazz musician and
    becoming a preacher.)

"Mahalia swings again, " 13:42-45, Mar. 1964.
    (Mahalia sings in the movie The Best Man.)

"Many faces of Ivan Dixon, " 14:32-36, July 1965.

"Most controversial Hollywood movie, " 6:65-69, May
1958.

"Most unusual standin, " 7:18-19, Dec. 1959.

"Negro playwright's classic becomes a movie, " A. S.
Young, 7:57-62, Apr. 1959.
    (Take a Giant Step.)

"New look in Hollywood, " A. S. Young, 7:30-34, Mar.
1959.
    ("The cards are falling right at last for talented
    Negro artists who have sought a break in films. ")

"Rafer Johnson: born to be a star, " 19:30-32, Feb.
1970.

"Raymond St. Jacques: a new meaning for 'superstar',"
19:62-65, Aug. 1970.

"Rebel with a cause: new lease on life for Billy

SEPIA (cont.)

Williams, " A. Duckett, 9:37-41, Mar. 1960.

"Naked Prey, " 15:66-70, Dec. 1966.

"Nat Cole's daughter seeks movie stardom, " 15:32-37,
June 1966.
(Carol Cole, working under contract to Columbia
Pictures.)

"The Pearl Bailey nobody knows, " Dorothy Black, 20:
54-61, Apr. 1971.

"Sad semi-secret death of a star: James Edwards'
death goes almost unnoticed by those he helped, " 19:
72-77, Mar. 1970.

"Sepia goes to a premier of Porgy and Bess, " D.
Hepburn, 7:8-14, Sept. 1959.

"Sexiest Hollywood actress since Lena Horne, " 12:36-
41, Jan. 1963.
(Mittie Lawrence).

"Sidney Poitier-Diahann Carroll, " 14:8-12", Jun. 1965.

"Sidney Poitier's fight with a nazi, " 11:41-44, Sept.
1962.

"Sins of Rachel Cade, " A. S. Young, 9:50-53, Jan.
1961.

"Soaring star called Mimi, " 13:42-46, Apr. 1964,
(Mimi Dillard.)

"Sudden stardom for James Earl Jones, " 18:52-55,
June 1969.

"Sue Schapiro, lady movie producer, " 19:32-36, Aug.
1970.

"Tamango, " 8:24-27, Jan. 1960.

"They live on the edge of Hollywood, " A. S. Young,
10:29-32, Nov. 1961.
("The Negro in Hollywood: standing on the edge,

hoping that training, luck will open doors. ")

"They made him a saint, " 16:60-63, Oct. 1967.
(Cuban actor Rene Munez, who played the part of
Saint Martin de Porres.)

"To Kill a Mockingbird, " 12:32-33, May 1963.

"To Sir, with Love, " 16:76-79, Apr. 1967.

"Tokyo's little mister star, " 9:38-40, Feb. 1961.
(Clinton Mumford, 12-year-old actor in a Japanese
production.)

"View from the top, " 15:49-53, Aug. 1970.
(Wendell Franklin and Horace Jackson, Black di-
rector and producer, respectively, discuss their
Hollywood careers.)

"Wanted: black talent; apply Hollywood, " 17:16-18,
Oct. 1968.

"What makes Ron Rich run?" 15:44-48, July 1966.

"Whatever Lola wants, Lola Falana gets, " 16:32-36,
Apr. 1967.

"Willie Davis: baseball player, natural actor, " 19:58-
63, May 1970.

"Woody Strode does it again, " 14:18-21, Aug. 1965.

SHOW

"Hollywood and the Black man, " Paul Ringo, Sept.
1972, p. 61.

SIGHT AND SOUND

"Negro films, " 18:27-30, Jan. 1950.
(Pinky, Home of the Brave, Lost Boundaries.)

SOCIAL PROBLEMS

"Straight with no cop-outs," 16:525-527, Spring '69.
(Analysis of two of Sidney Poitier's movies: Guess
Who's Coming to Dinner and Patch of Blue.)

SOUL ILLUSTRATED

"Black screen image," Walter Burrell, Feb. 1970,
pp. 19-20+.

THEATRE ARTS

"Negro in the American theatre: a record of achievement," 26:492-543, Aug. 1942.

TIME

"Black market," 99:53, Apr. 10, 1972.

"Boycott in Hollywood?" 70:90, Dec. 2, 1957.
(Porgy and Bess.)

"Cicely Tyson," 100:58, Oct. 9, 1972.

"Dark Laughter," 35:84, Apr. 29, 1940.
(Review of the film Mr. Washington Goes to Town.)

"The Green Pastures," 27:38-40, June 29, 1936.

"Hallelujah," 14:64, Sept. 2, 1929.

"Hollywood in the Bronx," 35:67, Jan. 29, 1940.
(The Micheaux Picture Corporation and its productions.)

"Power to the Peebles," 98:47, Aug. 16, 1971.
(Melvin Van Peebles.)

TUESDAY MAGAZINE

"The filmmakers: Focusing on History and present
status of Black filmmakers," Charles Hobson, 5:7-9,
Feb. 1970.

VARIETY WEEKLY

"Black actor William Marshall gives pedagogs low-down on 'coon' age, " Lee Beaupre, Aug. 15, 1973.

"Blaxploitationers of 1972, " Jan. 3, 1973.
(Summary of happenings in Black film in 1972.)

"Brock Peters on Negro skepticism, " Lee Beaupre, Dec. 20, 1967.

"Carmen Jones' box office click improves Negro casting chances, " Feb. 23, 1955.

"Columbia Pictures names Negro as a corporate officer," Aug. 20, 1969.
(George Marshall named assistant secretary of Columbia Pictures.)

"Columbia's Negro biz pitch, " Jan. 13, 1967, p. 7.

"Dorothy Dandridge's death recalls efforts to expand scope of roles for Negroes, " Sept. 15, 1965.

"8 Atlanta nabes admitting Negroes, " Aug. 7, 1963.

"Films, Poitier, and race riots, " Robert J. Landry, Jan. 3, 1968, p. 12.

"Fla. theatres racial policies still an issue, " Aug. 7, 1963.

"Goal: a Negro in every crew, " July 24, 1963.

"Hollywood NAACP in stepped up pitch for Negro film-TV production employment, " July 28, 1965.

"IATSE: no Negro need apply, " July 31, 1963, p. 7.

"If Poitier can't do it they rewrite for a white actor, " Robert B. Frederick, Oct. 4, 1964.

"Italy's film industry may top Hollywood in lifting bias as Negro roles soar, " June 12, 1968, p. 30.

"It's another part of the jungle: COMPO fears its civil rights confused with rights for Negroes, " Aug. 7, 1963.

VARIETY WEEKLY (cont.)

"Jewish museum's retrospective on Black filmmaking, back to 1916, " Mar. 25, 1970.

"Jim Brown may make it in pics, à la Poitier, " Jan. 24, 1968.

"Negro actors in Hollywood clover, " June 3, 1964.

"Negro actors win roles in German films, " July 31, 1963.

"Negro pioneers comment, " Dec. 27, 1967, p. 16.

"Negro 2d. assistant cameraman, " Oct. 13, 1963.

"Negro stop-and-go signs of 1964, " Jan. 6, 1965.

"Negroes and the boxoffice, " Nov. 29, 1967, p. 3.

"Negroes included as trainees at Metro and Revue-Universal, " July 17, 1963.

"Negroes into pix production, " May 19, 1965.

"One-third film public Negro, " Lee Beaupre, Nov. 29, 1967, p. 3.

"Q. T. boycott of Negro films, " Mar. 25, 1959.

"Rise of Negro matinee idol, " Robert H. Welker, Feb. 1, 1961, p. 7.

"South still snubs Negro films, " Apr. 7, 1954, p. 5.

"Violence overdone in Black capers, " Robert B. Frederick, Mar. 7, 1973.

VISION

"Stereotypes of Negroes in film, " 1:69, 1962.

WALL STREET JOURNAL

"Rights drive spurs casting of Negroes in movies, TV shows," Sept. 24, 1963.

WASHINGTON POST

"The Great White Hope," Gary Arnold, Dec. 31, 1970, p. C1.

"It's Your Thing," Sept. 3, 1970, p. C12.

"Sweetback," Gary Arnold, May 30, 1971, p. E3.

CHRONOLOGICAL LISTINGS

THROUGH THE TWENTIES

CHICAGO DEFENDER: "Within Our Gates, " Jan. 10, 1920,
p. 6.
(Oscar Micheaux production.)

CRISIS: "The Birth of a Nation, " 14:25-26, May 1917.

LITERARY DIGEST: "Primitive emotions aflame in a Negro
film, " 103:42-56, Oct. 5, '29.

NEW REPUBLIC: "The Birth of a Nation, " Francis Hackett,
2:185, Mar. 20, 1915.

THE THIRTIES

BROWN AMERICAN: "The Negro theatre, " 1:16+, Dec.
1936.

CATHOLIC WORLD: "A modern miracle play, " Euphemia
V. R. Wyatt. 131:210-11, May 1930.
(The Green Pastures.)

CHRISTIAN CENTURY: "Movies turn deaf ear to colored
plea, " 47:1140, Sept. 24, 1930.
(About Black protests of Birth of a Nation.)

CRISIS: "Uncle Tom in Hollywood, " Loren Miller. 41:329,
Nov. 1949.

"Hollywood's new Negro films, " Loren Miller. 45:8,
Jan. 1938.

ETUDE: "Worthwhile music in the movies; much choral

work done by Negro organization, " 57:152, Mar. 1939.

MOTION PICTURE HERALD: "Distributor lists Negro pictures, " Aug. 15, 1936.

"232 Negro theatres 1-1/2% of all houses, " Apr. 24,
1937.

OPPORTUNITY: "End of a controversy, " 13:231, Aug. 1935.
(About the film Imitation of Life.)

"Hollywood presents us, "   Cecil D. Halliburton.   13:296,
Oct, 1935.

TIME: "The Green Pastures, " 27:38-40, June 29, 1936.

THE FORTIES

CHICAGO DEFENDER: "A report on filmland, "   Walter
White.   May 8, 1943.

COLLIER'S: "Carmen Jones, " 113:14-15, Jan. 15, 1944.

DAILY VARIETY: "All-American newsreel, " Mar. 7, 1945.

EBONY: "How movies are made, " 2:40-43, Mar. 47.

"Hollywood debut for Pearl Bailey, " 2:38-39, Apr. 47.

"Canada Lee back in ring, " 2:16-17, Aug. 47.

"The Peanut Man, " 2:48-50, Jul. 47.

"The Burning Cross, " 2:36-41, Sept. 47.

"Black Gold, " 2:39, Oct. 47.

"Senza Pieta" [Without Pity], 4:62-65, Nov. 48.

"Knock on Any Door, " 4:34-38, Jan. 49.

"Movie debut, " (James Edwards), 4:25, Apr. 49.

"Any Number Can Play, " 4:24-26, May 49.

EBONY (cont.)

> "Home of the Brave, " 4:59-62, June 49.
>
> "Lost Boundaries, " 4:51-53, July 49.
>
> "Intruder in the Dust, " 4:25-28, Aug. 49.
>
> "Pinky, " 4:23-25, Sept. 49.
>
> "Movie choir, " (Jester Hairston Choir), 4:25-27, Oct. 49.
>
> "Secret of a movie maid, " 5:52-56+, Nov. 49.

HOLLYWOOD CITIZEN-NEWS: "Negro critics form group, " Nov. 19, 1949.

JOURNAL OF NEGRO EDUCATION: "Educational programs for the improvement of race relations, " 13:367-89, '44.

LOS ANGELES SENTINEL: "Negroes 'written out' of Hollywood movies, " May 9, 1946.

MOTION PICTURE HERALD: "Negroes movie-conscious; support 430 film houses, " Jan. 24, 1942, pp. 33-34.

> "Goldberg plans 12 Negro features, " (all-Black movies) Apr. 14, 1945.

NEGRO DIGEST: "The Negro and the movies, " William Harrison. #1 2:19-21, Aug. 40.

> "The Negro in show business, " 1:34 Feb. 43.
>
> "Is Hollywood fair to Negroes in its films?" 1:15-21, Apr. 43.
>
> "'De Lawd' cooks with gas, " (Rex Ingram) 2:53-33, Jan. 44.
>
> "Blackface, Hollywood style, " Dalton Trumbo. 2:37-39, Feb. 44.
>
> "Actors show how (editorial), " 2:63-64, Apr. 44.
>
> "Stardom 'for Negroes only', " Don Deleihbur. 3:87-88, Nov. 44.

NEGRO DIGEST (cont.)

"Tooting Lena's horn, " Charlotte Kay. 3:25-29, Aug. 45.

"Screen stereotypes, " Leon H. Hardwick. 4:57-58, May 46.

"Hollywood's new deal for Negroes, " John T. McManus and Louis Kronenberger. 4:77-80, Jun. 46.

"Negro lobby in Hollywood, " David O. Selznick, 4:27-28, Aug. 46.

"How Hollywood feels about Negroes, " Robert Jones. 5:4-8, Aug. 47.

"A Hollywood actress looks at the Negro, " Marshal Hunt. 5:14-17. Sept. 47.

"How Hollywood can better race relations, " John Garfield. 6:4-8, Nov. 47.

"Peck on prejudice, " Anne Strick. 6:17-20, July 48.

"Race tolerance: newest box office hit, " Peggy Weil. 6:46-49, Aug. 48.

NEW MASSES: "G'wan with the wind, " James Dugan. 34: 28, Jan. 2, 1940.

NEW YORK TIDINGS: "The sound track, " (column), William Mooring. June 2, 1944.

NEW YORK TIMES: "History of a dream, " W. E. B. Du Bois. Sept. 24, 1944.

OPPORTUNITY: "They made good in the movie capital, " William Smallwood. 19:76-77, Mar. 41.

PHYLON: "Hollywood report, " 6:13-16, Winter 45.

THEATRE ARTS: "The Negro in the American theatre: a record of achievement, " E. J. Isaacs. 26:492-543, Aug. 42.

TIME: "Hollywood in the Bronx, " 35:67, Jan. 29, 1940.

TIME (cont.)

>"Dark laughter, "   35:84,   Apr.   29,   1940.
>(Critique of film Mr. Washington Goes to Town.)

THE FIFTIES

COLOR: "Don Blackman's big role in Santiago, "   11:7-9,
Aug. 56.

COMMENTARY: "Two social scientists view No Way Out;
the unconscious vs. the message in an anti-bias film, "
Martha Wolfenstein and Nathan Leites.   10:388-91, Oct.
50.

CRISIS: "Angelitos Negros, "   57:221-225+, Apr. 50.

>"Mulatto, "   57:698-699, Dec. 50.

>"Old stereotyped pattern, "   George Yamada.   60:17-19,
>Jan. 53.

DAILY VARIETY: "Theatrical, TV film industries pledge to
depict Negroes 'as in real life', " Oct. 28, 1957.

EBONY: "Chicago slums are recreated in Buenos Aires for
film scenes: Wright explains ideas about movie making,"
6:84-85, Jan. 51.
(Native Son.)

>"Mexico's interracial movie" (Angelitos Negros.) 5:48-50,
>Feb. 50.

>"No Way Out, "   5:31-34, Mar. 50.

>"Lawless, "   5:59-62, May 50.

>"Jackie Robinson Story, "   5:87-88+, Jun. 50.

>"Lights Out, "   6:87-88+, Dec. 50.

>"Native Son filmed in Argentina, "   6:82-86, Jan. 51.

>"Steel Helmet, "   6:78-80, Mar. 51.

"Of Men and Music," 6:49-50+, May 51.

"Cry the Beloved Country," 6:57-62, July 51.

"Showboat: William Warfield makes film debut in revival," 6:69-71, Jan. 51.

"Businessmen push fair job drive," 6:15-18+, Aug. 51.

"Pool of London," 6:59-61, Oct. 51.

"Lydia Bailey," 7:39-44, Jan. 52.

"Movie musicals; ranking Negro performers given musical bits in half-dozen coming Hollywood productions," 6:51-53, Aug. 51.

"Stepin Fetchit comes back," 7:64-67, Feb. 52.

"Glory Alley," 7:100-102+, May 52.

"From film actor to college prof," (Juano Hernandez), 8:122-126, Nov. 52.

"Member of the Wedding: Ethel Waters," 8:47-51, Dec. 52.

"President's Lady; Vera Francis gets explosive role in movie touching on mixed romance theme," 8:71-75, Feb. 53.

"Anna's Sin," 9:33-36, Mar. 53.

"French movie star: Moune de Rivel ... stars in new film touching on racial bias," 8:103-108, Mar. 53.

"See How They Run," 8:43-46+, Apr. 53.

"Mambo," 10:83-84+, Dec. 54.

"I came back from the dead," (Rex Ingram), 10:49-52, Mar. 55.

"Blackboard Jungle: Sidney Poitier has key role in brutal film about teacher, juvenile delinquents," 10:87-88, May 55.

EBONY (cont.)

"Dorothy Dandridge's greatest triumph," 10:37-41, July 55.

"Madi Comfort: newest movie queen," 10:25-28, Sept. 55.

"Moby Dick," 10:107-109, Sept. 55.

"Pete Kelly's Blues: Ella Fitzgerald draws a hot jazz assignment for her first major role in movies," 10:115-117, Oct. 55.

"Do Negroes have a future in Hollywood?" 11:24, Dec. 55.

"Trial," 11:29-30+, Nov. 55.

"Simba," 11:73-76, Jan. 56.

"Harder They Fall: Joe Walcott is convincing actor in first movie role," 11:87-90, May 56.

"High Society: new movie with jazz angle has role made for Satchmo," 11:103-105, July 56.

"Dandridge gets red carpet treatment," 11:24, Aug. 56.

"Miss Waters regrets," 12:56-60, Feb. 57.

"Jedda," 12:108+, Mar. 57.

"Crooner Nat 'King' Cole turns actor," 12:74, Jun. 57.

"Island in the Sun," 12:32-34+, July 57.

"Movie features blossoming star," 13:93-94, Nov. 57.

"A pooped Pearlie Mae," 13:55-56, Apr. 58.

"St Louis Blues: Nat 'King' Cole plays lead role in film biography of W. C. Handy," 13:27-28, May 58.

"A star at ten," (Darrell Harris), 13:59, July 58.

"The Defiant Ones," 13:80, Oct. 58.

"Miss Dunham trains dancers for new film," (Green Mansions), 13:121-122, Oct. 58.

"Decks Ran Red: in eighth movie, Dorothy Dandridge displays acting skill," 14:60-62, Nov. 58.

"Anna Lucasta: Eartha Kitt, Sammy Davis star in film," 14:72-76, Dec. 58.

"Sportin' life and the strange 'lady'," 14:97-98, Feb. 59.

"Grace through exercise," 14:33-36, Mar. 59. (Dorothy Dandridge.)

"Imitation of Life: Juanita Moore stars in new version of film," 14:70-73, Apr. 59.

"Hollywood's first Negro movie star: Sidney Poitier breaks film barrier to become screen idol," Lerone Bennett, Jr. 14:100-103, May 59.

"Your Very Own: homeless children find new parents, new lives," 14:113-114, May 59.

"Althea's film debut," 14:73-74, July 59. (Althea Gibson.)

"Movie maker Belafonte," 14:94-96, July 59.

"Anatomy of a Murder: Hollywood uses talents of Duke Ellington in movie," 14:106-108, Sept. 59.

"Dandridge marries; simple wedding is movieland wonder," 14:135-138, Sept. 59.

"Take a Giant Step: singer Johnny Nash makes debut as actor," 14:48-51, Sept. 59.

"I didn't want to play a bigot," Robert Ryan, 15:68-70+, Nov. 59.

"Actor Satch; ageless hurler plays cavalry sergeant," 15:109-110, Dec. 59. (Satchel Paige.)

"Sapphire," 15:51-54+, Dec. 59.

EBONY (cont.)

> "Movie starlet's Roman holiday, " (Tessa Prendergast), 10:27-30+, Jan. 50.

> "Sailor to movie star: Japanese problem film makes star of Navy's Danny Williams, " 8:46-51, Aug. 53.

> "Star of Italian movies: John Kitzmiller, " 7:71-73, Nov. 51.

> "Why Negroes don't like Eartha Kitt, " 10:29-38, Dec. 54.

FILM QUARTERLY: "Beige, brown or Black, " Albert Johnson, 13:38-43, Fall 59.

FILMS AND FILMING: "The Negro in cinema, " 3:9-11, May 57.

> "How Hollywood is smashing the color bar, " Sidney Harmon, 5:7+, Mar. 59.

FILMS IN REVIEW: "The Negro films today, " Arthur Knight, Feb. 50, pp. 14-19.

HOLLYWOOD REPORTER: "Negro actors hit 'Red front' meet, " June 13, 1952.

> "Reds map Negro agitation, " June 16, 1952.

> "Studio films schedules 12 featurettes, " June 12, 1955.

> "New producing unit for Negro talent, " Oct. 3, 1955.

LIBERATION: "He who must die, " 4:17-18, Mar. 59.

LOS ANGELES DAILY NEWS: "Top Negro actors rap ASPC meet here as 'Red promoted', " June 13, 1952.

LOS ANGELES EXAMINER: "Negro actors tell stand on ASP meeting, " June 13, 1952.

NEGRO DIGEST: "She passed for Negro--in the movies, " (Jeanne Crain,) 8:26-27, Mar. 50.

> "Do you remember 'Our Gang'?" 9:69-70, Dec. 50.

"Hollywood director speaks out," Robert Ellis. 9:42-44, Jan. 51.

"He passed as a Negro," Al Weisman. 9:16-20, Oct. 51.
(Mel Ferrer.)

"Ida Lupino brings new hope to Hollywood," Robert Ellis. 8:47-49, Aug. 50.

"Movie star who hates his job," (Richard Widmark), Robert Ellis. 9:81-83, Dec. 50.

NEGRO HISTORY BULLETIN: "Passing years," 22:93-94, Jan. 59.

NEW YORK TIMES: "Red slant," May 20, 1951.

OUR WORLD: "Lena Horne: Our World's first cover girl," 5:11-13, Apr. 50.

"Without Pity," 5:37, May 50.

"The Breaking Point (Juano Hernandez)," 5:51, Aug. 50.

"Native Son," 5:36-38, Dec. 50.

"Cry the Beloved Country: visiting actors taste South Africa's race hate while making movie," 6:34-36, July 51.

"Pool of London," 6:43-45, Sept. 51.

"The Well: false kidnapping is theme of thrilling film," 6:58-59, Oct. 51.

"Red Ball Express," 7:42-43, Apr. 52.

"Can Dandridge outshine Lena Horne?" 7:29-32, June 52.

"Haiti goes to the movies," (Lydia Bailey) 7:46-53, Aug. 52.

"ABC's of movieland," Gertrude Gipson, 7:60-64, Sept. 52.

"What's cookin' in Hollywood?" 7:62-63, Oct. 52.

OUR WORLD (cont.)

"Jamaica Sea" (Bill Walker), 7:60-61, Dec. 52.

"The passing of Beulah: Will Hattie McDaniel's death
mark end of long era of 'kitchen-comedy' roles for Negroes on radio and screen?" 8:12-15, Deb. 53.

"Vera Francis; movies' new sex thrill, " 8:54-57, Mar.
53.

"Aftermath: here is Marva .... " 8:12-13, July 53.

"Hollywood ... so what!" James Edwards. 8:56-59,
Dec. 53.

"Bill Marshall: matinee idol, " 9:38-41, Feb. 54.

"Mme Sul-Te-Wan: at 80, she's the oldest Negro actress
in Hollywood, " 9:80-82, Feb. 54.

"Strange love story; Negro movie company with ... story
on color prejudice among Negroes themselves, " 9:26-28,
Mar. 54.

PHYLON: "The problem of Negro character and dramatic
incident, " William Couch, Jr. 127-133, Jun. 50.

"Pro-Negro films in Atlanta, " Gerald Weales. (re-
print from Films in Review, Nov. 52), 13:298-304. Dec.
52.

"How genuine is The Green Pastures?" Nick Aaron
Ford. 20:67-70. Spring 59.

"The Green Pastures again, " Doris H. Garey. 20:193-
194, Summer 59.

QUARTERLY OF FILM, RADIO, AND TELEVISION: "The
film gains a new dimension, " Jack Howard. 7:77, Fall
52.

QUICK NEWS WEEKLY: "The Negro in entertainment, "
Aug. 13, 1951.

SEPIA: "New look in Hollywood, " A. S. Young. 7:30-34,
Mar. 59.

"Negro playwright's classic becomes a movie, " A. S.
Young. 7:57-62, Apr. 59.
(Take a Giant Step.)

"Harry Belafonte's debut as a Hollywood producer, "
A. S. Young. 7:34-39. July 1959.

"Sepia goes to premier of Porgy and Bess, " D. Hepburn, 7:8-14, Sept. 59.

SIGHT AND SOUND: "Negro films, " 18:27-30, Jan. 50.

TIME: "Boycott in Hollywood?" 70:90, Dec. 2, 1959.
      (Porgy and Bess.)

VARIETY WEEKLY: "South still snubs Negro films, " Apr.
7, 1954, p. 5.

"Carmen Jones' boxoffice click improves Negro casting
chances, " Feb. 23, 1955.

"Q. T. boycott of Negro films, " Mar. 25, 1959, p. 17.

THE SIXTIES

AMERICA: "Negro actors in dramatic roles, " 115:298-300,
Sept. 17, 1966.

CHRISTIAN CENTURY: "NCOMP charges Hollywood lacks
black sensitivity, " 86:1157, Sept. 10, 1969.

COMMONWEAL: "Guess who's coming to lunch?" Philip T.
Hartung. 88:59, Aug. 23, 1968.

CORONET: "Negro and white love scenes that shock-it-to-
you!" Apr. 1969, pp. 10-17.

DAILY VARIETY: "(Darryl) Zanuck pledges fair 20th shake
in casting Negroes, " Oct. 4, '62.

"Definite increase in Hollywood jobs for Negro performers
reported, " Aug. 21, 1963.

"After 'big scare' Hollywood using darkest Negroes
around, " Oct. 11, 1963.

DAILY VARIETY (cont.)

"Token use of Negroes in pix and television could be dangerous, " Dave Kaufman, Jan. 23, 1969.

"Hollywood and the Negro musician, " Henry Roth. Feb. 17, 1964, p. 12.

"Negro actors org. disputes Wilkins view of Hollywood, " Dec. 9, 1964.

"Hollywood hitching no vehicles to current hot headlines of U. S. racial tensions, " Mar. 12, 1965.

"Thesps from racial minorities getting 8-9% of roles in Hollywood pix and television, " A. D. Murphy. Mar. 14, 1966.

"Goldwyn Jr. Negro feature series to star (Raymond) St. Jacques, (Godfrey) Cambridge, and (Calvin) Lockhart. "

"Smith first Negro dialog coach, " Apr. 9, 1968.

"NAACP to mount drive in June for more jobs in pix, " May 5, 1965.

"Valenti lauds Hyman for hiring Negro director, " May 13, 1968.

"More Italo pic parts for U. S. Negroes, " June 7, 1968.

"Pix gains 'disappoint' NAACP, " A. D. Murphy. July 23, 1965.

EBONY: "American in Italian movies, " 15:85-86+, June 60.

"Why I played Jim the slave, " Archie Moore. 15:43-44+, Sept. 60.

"Tony Curtis photographs Sergeants Three, " 17:43-44+, Apr. 62.

"Private world of Dorothy Dandridge, " 17:116-121, June 62.

"Why I played a film bigot, " Bobby Darin. 18:45-46+, Nov. 62.

"Lena Horne speaks freely on race, marriage, stage, "
Robert Feinstein.   18:61-67, May 63.

"Teenagers win movie roles, "   18:150-152, May 63.
(Judy Pace.)

"Brock Peters, "   18:106-112, June 63.

"Yank movie man of Japan, "   (Arthur "Chico" Lourant),
18:45-46+, July 63.

"100 years of Negro entertainment, "   Allan Morrison.
18:122-4, Sept. 63.

"Why the stars go broke, "   18:84-88, Sept. 63.

"Brando fights for civil rights, "   18:60-62+, Oct. 63.

"James Earl Jones: actor still climbing, "   20:98-106,
Apr. 65.

"New bad guy of the movies, "   (Raymond St. Jacques),
22:171-172+, June 67.

"Sidney Poitier: the man behind the star, "   Charles
Sanders.   23:171-174+, Apr. 68.

"The story of a three-day pass, "   23:54-60, Sept. 68.

"Uptight; film starring a Black anti-hero, "   24:46-48,
Nov. 68.

"Football heroes invade Hollywood, "   24:195-197, Oct. 69.

"Raymond the magnificent, "   (Raymond St. Jacques)
Charles Sanders.   25:175-178+, Nov. 69.

ENTERTAINMENT WORLD: "Hollywood in glorious Black
    and white, "   Leonard Feather.   Dec. 12, 1969.

FILM DAILY: "Negroes still given racially oriented pic
    roles: O. Davis, "   Allen C. Lobsenz.   Oct. 1, 1965.

    "Burt Lancaster sees Negro advance in films, "   Mar. 1,
    1968.

FILM QUARTERLY: "The Negro in American films: some

FILM QUARTERLY (cont.)

　　recent works, "　18:14-30, Summer 65.

FILM-TV DAILY:　"No color line in casting: (Jim) Brown and Raquel Welch, "　May 24, 1968.

　　"'Black America' focus on Hollywood influence, "　June 25, 1968.

FREEDOMWAYS:　"The Negro in American films, "　Carlton Moss.　3:134-142, Spr. 63.

HISTORIAN:　"Reaction of the Negro to the motion picture Birth of a Nation, "　25:344-362, May 63.

HOLLYWOOD CITIZEN-NEWS:　"Film stars and Negroes, "　Aug. 23, 1963.

　　"Hollywood lauded on Negro hiring, "　Dec. 2, 1964.

　　"Negro film roles show sharp increase, "　Apr. 22, 1969.

　　"Movie boycott threat, "　Oct. 9, 1969.

　　"NCI director says report lied, only 1 Black trainee hired, "　Jin Newsom.　Oct. 14, 1969.

HOLLYWOOD REPORTER:　"Central hires Negro, "　July 13, 1967.

　　"Color bar dissolves on selling, Negro actors find, "　Bob Hull.　May 6, 1968.

　　"Producers suggests Negro job center, "　Apr. 21, 1967.

　　"This may be year industry makes itself clear as far as Negro is concerned, says Brock Peters, "　Feb. 12, 1968.

　　"Negro actors should act, not be diverted, says Yaphet Kotto, "　June 4, 1968.

　　"Gordon Parks tells of union aid on Learning, "　Aug. 14, 1969.

　　"Brown outlines Black union plans 'self-determination',"

Collette Wood.   (Jim Brown.)   Aug. 26, 1969.

"Lou Rawls stars in first all-Black cowboy movie, "
Collette Wood.   Sept. 17, 1969.

JET: "The cry of jazz: Negro produced and directed documentary film depicting through jazz the Negro's struggle
..., " p. 62, Feb. 18, '60.

"U. S. Equal Employment Opportunity Commission calls
for job bias suit against giant movie makers, "   35:58-
59, Apr. 3, 1969.

JOURNAL OF THE PRODUCER'S GUILD OF AMERICA:
"Actors and other minority groups, "   Charlton Heston.
10:35-37, Mar. 68.

LIBERATOR: "The Black boom, "   4:16+, Aug. 64.

LOS ANGELES HERALD EXAMINER: "The honest movies
about Negroes--when?"   Renata Adler.   Mar. 3, 1968.

"Black comedy any answer in the ghetto?"   Mar. 31,
1968, p. C11.

"Jail threat, "   Aug. 23, 1963.

LOS ANGELES TIMES: "Four actors address Negro rally in
Alabama, "   Aug. 23, 1963.

"Ancient film's effect on modern Negro life, "   Roy
Wilkins.   (The Birth of a Nation), Feb. 15, 1965.

"Another kind of Negro stereotype, "   Hal Humphrey.
Apr. 13, 1967, pt. 5, p. 20.

"Award goes to Negro for movie work, "   Apr. 19, 1965.

"Hollywood gives more work, roles to Negro, "   Harry
Bernstein.   Mar. 13, 1966.

"Negro employment increases in films, "   Gene Handsaker.
Sept. 11, 1967.

"Can a 'laff riot' cure the other kind?"   Patricia E.
Davis.   Mar. 31, 1968.

LOS ANGELES TIMES (cont.)

   "Take two of a movie miracle, " Art Seidenbaum. Jan.
   6, 1968, pt. 3, p. 1.

   "Re-evaluation needed in film industry, " Charles Champlin.   Apr. 9, 1968, pt. 4, p. 1.

   "Film executive blames hiring bias on unions, " Robert
   Kistler. Oct. 19, 1969.

   "U. S. plans to prod film industry on job discrimination
   charge, " Vincent T. Burke. Oct. 19, 1969.

LOS ANGELES TIMES CALENDAR: "Hollywood's Negroes
   mired in stereotypes, " Burt Prelutsky.   Feb. 19, 1967,
   p. 9.

   "An assessment of the status of Hollywood Blacks, " Dan
   Knapp.   Sept. 28, 1969.

MOTION PICTURE EXHIBITOR: "Three Negroes convicted
   in N. C. trespass case, " Jan. 22, 1964.

MOTION PICTURE HERALD: "Race talks in Hollywood, "
   Aug. 7, 1963.

NEGRO DIGEST: "Why I became an actor, "   (Sidney Poitier)
   11:80-97, Dec. 61.

   "Negro in the American theater, "   11:52-58, July 62.

   "Needed: a Negro film movement, " Walter Moore. 15:
   45-48, Jan. 66.

   "Problems facing Negro actors, " Woodie King, Jr. 15:
   53-59, Apr. 66.

   "The tattered queens; some reflections on the Negro
   actress, " Ruby Dee. 15:32-36, Apr. 66.

   "Young actor on the way up: James Earl Jones, " Robert
   Burg.   15:26-31, Apr. 66.

   "Hollywood and the Negro: the slow pace of change, "
   Robert G. Hunter.   15:37-41, May 66.

"Movies in the ghetto B. P. (before Poitier), " 18:21-27, Fall 69.

NEGRO HISTORY BULLETIN: "'Hollywood phony on Negro films', writer charges, " p. 21, Oct. 60.

"The image makers: Negro stereotypes, " 26:127-128, Dec. 62.

"Enroute to the future, " 30:13, Apr. 67.

"Not by protest alone!" 31:12-14, Apr. 68.

NEW YORK TIMES: "Stars join drive against bigotry, " July 15, 1963.

"Mayor in Alabama rebuffs four actors, " Aug. 24, 1963.

"Hollywood acts on race problem, " Sept. 21, 1963, p. 8L.

"Hollywood change: Negroes gain in a new movie and elsewhere, " Larry Glen. Sept. 22, 1963.

"The Negro in films, " Bosley Crowther. Oct. 6, 1963.

"The Negro in films: Poitier points a dilemma which The Cool World helps rebut, " Apr. 26, 1964.

"The still invisible man, " Peter Bart. July 17, 1966.

"Why does white America love Sidney Poitier so?" Clifford Mason. Sept. 10, 1967, p. 1.

"The Negro actor asks himself: 'Am I a Negro or am I an Actor?'" Walter Kerr. 34-5, Oct. 15, 1967.

"About Negro directors, " Dec. 24, 1967.

"To make the Negro a living human being, " Lindsay Patterson. Feb. 18, 1968, p. 8D.

"Belafonte: 'Look, " they tell me, 'don't rock the boat'," Harry Belafonte. Apr. 21, 1968.

"Hollywood's boy and girl next door--color them white, " Lindsay Patterson. June 16, 1968, p. D9.

PHYLON: "Death of Rastus: Negroes in American films
    since 1945, "   28:267-275.   Fall 67.

SATURDAY REVIEW: "The problem, " Hollis Alpert.   50:
    50, Jan. 21, 1967.

SEPIA: "Wonderful Country, "   8:44-50, Feb. 60.

    "Rebel with a cause: new lease on life for Billy Wil-
    liams, "   9:37-41, Mar. 60.

    "Sepia visits a filming, "   A. S. Young. 8:56-61, June
    60.

    "Great athlete finds Hollywood stardom, "   A. S. Young.
    8:64-67, Aug. 60.
    (Woody Strode.)

    "Tokyo's little mister star, "   M. Goodwin, A. Brown.
    9:38-40, Feb. 61.

    "They live on the edge of Hollywood, "   A. S. Young.
    10:29-32, Nov. 61.

    "Diahann Carroll: talented bombshell, "   11:57-59, Mar.
    62.

    "Athlete Rafer Johnson becomes top Hollywood star, "
    11:58-62, June 62.

    "Sidney Poitier's fight with a Nazi, "   11:44, Sept. 62.

    "How liberal is show business?"   12:40-43, Mar. 63.

    "Hollywood hires a Negro director, "   12:35-38, Apr. 63.
    (Wendell Franklin.)

    "Hollywood's new breed, "   12:20-25, June 63.

    "James Earl Jones' goal is to become great actor, "   13:
    72-76, Feb. 64.

    "Living between two worlds, "   13:62-66, Feb. 64.

    "Mahalia swings again, "   13:42-45, Mar. 64.

    "Barbara McNair, "   13:74-78, Apr. 64.

"Soaring star called Mimi, "   13:42-46, Apr. 64.

"How Sidney Poitier won an oscar, "   13:14-17, June 64.

"Jim Brown in Rio Conchos, "   13:22-25, Dec. 64.

"Sidney Poitier - Diahann Carroll, "   14:8-12+, June 65.

"Many faces of Ivan Dixon, "   14:32-36, July 65.

"Woody Strode does it again, "   14:18-21, Aug. 65.

"Life and death of Dorothy Dandridge, " A. S. Young.
14:8-12+, Dec. 65.

"Nat Cole's daughter seeks movie stardom, "   15:32-37,
June 66.

"What makes Ron Rich run?"   15:44-48, July 66.

"Ivan Dixon at home, "   16:38-41, Feb. 67.

"Whatever Lola wants, Lola Falana gets, "   16:32-36,
Apr. 67.

"They made him a saint, "   16:60-63, Oct. 67.

"Wanted: Black talent; apply Hollywood, " 17:16-18, Oct.
68.

"Sudden stardom for James Earl Jones, "   18:52-55,
June 69.

"Is Hollywood afraid to star a sexy Black actress?"
18:10-15, June 69.

"Do Black actors make good fathers?"   18:32-34, Dec.
69.

SOCIAL PROBLEMS: "Straight with no cop-outs, "   16:525-7,
Spring 69.

VARIETY WEEKLY: "Rise of Negro matinee idol, " Robert
H. Welker.   Feb. 1, 1961, p. 7.

"Negroes included as trainees at Metro and Revue-Universal, " July 17, 1963.

VARIETY WEEKLY (cont.)

"Goal: a Negro in every crew, "   July 24, 1963.

"IATSE: no Negro need apply, "   July 31, 1963, p. 7.

"Negro actors win roles in German films, "   July 31, 1963.

"8 Atlanta nabes admitting Negroes, "   Aug. 7, 1963.

"Fla. theatres racial policies still an issue, "   Aug. 7, 1963.

"It's another part of the jungle: COMPO fears its civil rights confused with rights for Negroes, "   Aug. 7, 1963.

"Negro 2d. assistant cameraman, "   Oct. 13, 1963.

"Negro actors in Hollywood clover, "   June 3, 1964.

"If Poitier can't do it they rewrite for a white actor, " Robert B. Frederick.   Oct. 4, 1964.

"Negro stop-and-go signs of 1964, "   Jan. 6, 1965.

"Negroes into pix production, "   May 19, 1965.

"Hollywood NAACP in stepped up pitch for Negro film-TV production employment, "   July 28, 1965.

"Dorothy Dandridge's death recalls efforts to expand scope of roles for Negroes, "   Sept. 15, 1965.

"Columbia's Negro biz pitch, "   Jan. 13, 1967, p. 7.

"Negroes and the box office, "   Nov. 29, 1967.

"One-third film public Negro, "   Lee Beaupre.   Nov. 29, 1967, p. 3.

"Brock Peters on Negro skepticism, "   Lee Beaupre. Dec. 20, 1967.

"Negro pioneers comment, "   Dec. 27, 1967.

"Films, Poitier, and race riots, "   Robert J. Landry.

Jan. 3, 1968, p. 12.

"Jim Brown may make it in pics, à la Poitier," Jan.
24, 1968.

"Italy's film industry may top Hollywood in lifting bias
as Negro roles soar," June 12, 1968, p. 30.

"Columbia Pictures names Negro as a corporate officer,"
(George Marshall named assistant secretary of Columbia
Pictures), Aug. 20, 1969.

VISION: "Stereotypes of Negroes in film," 1:69, '62.

WALL STREET JOURNAL: "Rights drive spurs casting of
Negroes in movies, television shows," Sept. 24, 1963.

THE SEVENTIES

AMERICA: "More about Black films," 127:459-60, Nov. 25,
1972.

AMERICAN FILM INSTITUTE: "The silent minority,"
Stephen Zito. pp. 2-3, May 71.
(Early Black film companies and their productions.)

BLACK CREATION: "The independents: hard road for the
old and new," 3:8-11, Spr. 72.

"Clayton Riley on the Black critic," 3:15, Summer 72.

"West coast gets the Shaft," 3:12-14, Summer 72.

"William Greaves: creatively independent," 4:10-11,
Fall 72.

"St. Claire Bourne: alternative Black visions," Michael
Mattox. 4:32-34, Summer 73.
(Chamba Productions, Inc.)

"The day Black movie stars got militant," 4:40, Winter
73.

"Director Ossie Davis talks about Black Girl," 4:38-39,
Winter 73.

BLACK CREATION (cont.)

> "Expanding world of the Black film (editorial), " 4:25, Winter 73.

> "Film as a tool for liberation?" 4:36-37, Winter 73.

> "A futuristic fable, " 4:43, Winter 73.

> "History lesson: the boom is really an echo, " 4:32-34, Winter 73.

> "The subject is money, " 4:26, Winter 73.

> "The ten most important Black films between 1962 and 1972 (list), " Vol. 4 #2, Winter 73.

> "The Black woman as a sex image in films, " Walter Burrell. 2:32-39, Dec. 72.

BOX OFFICE: "Black film festival now offered in Indianapolis, " May 14, 1973.

BUSINESS SCREEN: "A concerned filmmaker, " Sept. 70. (William Greaves.)

CINEMA: "Black American cinema: A primer, " Norman Kagan. 6:2, Fall 70.

CINEMEDITOR: "It could only happen in jolly Hollywood, " Fall 70.

COMMONWEAL: "Era of dummies and darkies, " Stephen Fay. 93:125-8, Oct. 30, 1970.

> "Black and white: the screen, " Colin L. Westerbeck, Jr. 96:285-6, May 26, 1972.

DAILY VARIETY: "Black pic cycle mushrooming, " 157:1, Sept. 14, 1972.

> "Blaxploitation groups vows fight vs. film industry, " 157:1, Sept. 14, 1972.

> "O' Neal defends Superfly, " 157:1, Sept. 14, 1972.

> "Whitney Young urges Blacks set up their own production

companies, " Nov. 6, 1970.

"Griffin bails out of Blaxploitation Coalition post, " Aug. 1, 1972.

"(Black films): many of 50 planned may not materialize, but 20 actually being developed, " Aug. 14, 1972.

DRAMA REVIEW: "Black movies/Black theater, " James Murray. 16:56-61, Dec. 72.

EBONY: "King, from Montgomery to Memphis, " 25:172-174, Apr. 70.

"From model to movie star, " (Richard Roundtree.) 26: 128, June 71.

"Expanding world of Sidney Poitier, " L. Robinson. 27: 1-11$_+$, Nov. 71.

"Hollywood stunt girl, " (Peaches Jones.) 27:147-148+, Dec. 71.

"Trina Parks: the girl who zaps James Bond, " 27:68-70, Mar. 72.

"Black cinema expo. '72; Black cinema literary-research center, " 27:151-4, May 72.

"The Black man as movie hero; new films offer a different male image, " Theophilus Green. 27:144-148, Aug. 72.

"New films: culture or con game?" 28:60-62, Dec. 72.

"Looking back on blacks in films, " 28:35-44A, June 73.

"Battle among the beauties, " 29:144-45, Nov. 73.

ENCORE: "Which way the Black film?" 2:52-54, Jan. 73.

"Otto Preminger on Black movies, " 2:56-59, Aug. 73.

ESSENCE: "Buck and the Preacher, " 3:8, Aug. 72.

"A flood of Black films, " 5:28, Sept. 72.

ESSENCE (cont.)

"Gordon Parks, " 3:62, Oct. 72.

"Black imagery on the silver screen, " 3:34, Dec. 72.

"Ain't 'Beulah' dead yet? or images of the Black woman in film, " 4:61+, May 73.

"Paul Winfield: a man unto himself, " 4:27+, June 73.

"A bad Black image in film, " 4:70, May 73.

"Van Peebles on the inside, " 4:36+, June 73.

FILM CULTURE: "Tribute to Paul Robeson, " Fall, Winter 70.

FILM QUARTERLY: "Stepin Fetchit talks back; interview, " 24:20-6, Summer 71.

FILM-TV DAILY: "Non-acting film, video jobs for Blacks up 48% in 1969, " Vance King.   Mar. 12, 1970.

HOLLYWOOD CITIZEN-NEWS: "Writer says Blacks need own film heroes, " (Joe Greene, creator of "Super-spade".)   May 15, 1970.

HOLLYWOOD REPORTER: "Black capitalism big factor in PUSH drive on Hollywood, " Aug. 18, 1970.

"Black vise tightens: demand censorship on Black pictures, " Will Tusher.   Sept. 20, 1972.

"PUSH study shows systematic black-out of Blacks continues, " Nov. 8, 1972.

"Raymond St. Jacques claims critics pamper Black films, " Ron Pennington.   Jan. 8, 1973, p. 13.

"Peters forms Black production company, sets initial projects, " Mar. 20, 1973.
(Thomas Peters, founder of Indepth Productions.)

"Black producers mass to generate financing, " Will Tusher.   June 29, 1973, p. 1.

"Black backers set hard line: big demand for film dollar," Ron Pennington. Nov. 7, 1973, p. 3.

JET: "Public finally to see documentary on Angela Davis," 41-47, Nov. 25, 1971.

"Sidney Poitier makes relevant film for Blacks," C. S. Thompson. 41:58-61, May 13, 1971.

"Strode is brilliant as 'Black Jesus'," 41:53, Oct. 7, 1971.

JOURNAL OF RELIGIOUS THOUGHT: "Secular prophecy in an age of film," 27:63-75, Spr-Sum. 70.

LIFE: "Black Hollywood," Jan. 23, 1970. pp. M19-M21.

"Real anger was backstage; racial tensions during shooting of Halls of Anger, 69:50-2, Aug. 21, 1970.

"Films for Blacks," Richard Schickel. 72:20, June 72.

LOOK: "Poitier meets Belafonte," George Goodman. 35:56-60, Aug. 24, 1971.
(Review of Buck and the Preacher.)

LOS ANGELES SENTINEL: "Karate champion Jim Kelly makes movie debut," Sept. 6, 1973, p. B2A.

"A super star in Maurie: Bernie Casey," Sept. 6, '73. p. B1A.

"Celebrity marriage," Gertrude Gipson. Sept. 20, '73, p. A1.

"Lady Sings the Blues," Oct. 4, '73, p. B1A. (Diana Ross.)

"Hell Up in Harlem stars Fred Williamson," Oct. 11, '73, p. B7.

"Pam Grier is Foxy Brown," Oct. 11, '73, p. B6.

"Jesse Jackson applauds Save the Children," Oct. 25, '73, p. B9.

LOS ANGELES TIMES: "Don Williams, "   Mary Murphy.
    Mar. 24, 1973.

    "I wish mom could see me now, "   Skip Ferderber.
    Nov. 22, '73, pt. 4, p. 36.

LOS ANGELES TIMES CALENDAR: "Makers of Black films
    stand at crossroads, "   Jan. 28, '73.   p. 18.

MASSACHUSETTS REVIEW: "Paul Robeson and Black identity
    in American films, "   11:468-85, Summer 70.

MOVIE/TV MARKETING: "Guess who's coming to cinema?"
    Edward Mapp.   24:44 Mar. 70.

NATIONAL REVIEW: "Superspade's revenge, "   5:39-40, May
    12, 1972.

NEGRO HISTORY BULLETIN: "Return of 'The Emperor
    Jones', "   34:160-2, Nov. 71.

    "Dark horse operas: a film article, "   36:13-14, Jan. 73.

NEW REPUBLIC: "Stanley Kaufmann on films, "   168:20+,
    Apr. 28, 1973.

NEW YORK TIMES: "So now I'm back and Black and avail-
    able, "   Peter De Anda.   Oct. 10, 1971.

    "Is it better to be Shaft than Uncle Tom?"   Aug. 26,
    1973, p. D11.

NEW YORKER: "Black film: God's step children, "   46:34-
    5, Apr. 18, 1970.

    "Notes on Black movies, "   48:159-65, Dec. 2, 1972.

NEWSWEEK: "Black movie boom, "   78:66, Sept. 6, 1971.

    "Blacks vs. Shaft, "   80:88, Aug. 28, 1972.

    "Black movies: renaissance or ripoff?"   80:74-8, Oct.
    23, 1972.

NORFOLK JOURNAL AND GUIDE: "MGM creates a Black
    star, "   (Richard Roundtree.)   Apr. 10, 1071, p. 14.

PHYLON: "Prejudicial film: progress and stalemate, 1915-
67, " Anne K. Nelsen and Hart M. Nelsen.   31:142-7,
Summer 70.

PITTSBURGH COURIER: "Talented Alex Clarke is a bold
Black actor, " Jan. 10, 1970, p. 12.

POLITICAL SCIENCE QUARTERLY: "Gamut from A to B:
the image of the Black in pre-1915 movies, " D. J.
Leab.   88:53-70, Mar. 73.

READER'S DIGEST: "Three lives of Ethel Waters, "   101:81-
85, Dec. 72.

SATURDAY REVIEW, ARTS: "First Black movie stars; excerpts from Toms, Coons, Mulattoes, Mammies and
Bucks (D. Bogle), "   1:25-9, Feb. 73.

SENIOR SCHOLASTIC: "Black films: values, pro and con, "
101:8-9, Dec. 11, 1972.

SEPIA: "Rafer Johnson: born to be a star, "   19:30-32,
Feb. 70.

"Janet Maclachlan grabs filmland's brass ring, "   19:54-
58, Mar. 70.

"Sad semi-secret death of a star. " (James Edwards),
19:72-77, Mar. 70.

"The Black path to Hollywood, " (Gordon Parks), 19:50-
52₊, Apr. 70.

"Willie Davis: baseball player, natural actor, " 19:58-63,
May 70.

"Allison Mills, " W. Jenkins.   19:14-17, July 70.

"Raymond St. Jacques: a new meaning for 'superstar', "
19:62-65, Aug. 70.

"Beauty that is Barbara McNair, "   19:72-73, Nov. 70.

"James Earl Jones: race is still the important thing, "
20:16-17, Jan. 71.

"The Pearl Bailey nobody knows, " Doris Black.   20:54-

SEPIA (cont.)

 61, Apr. 71.

 "Black playboy of Hollywood, " (Raymond St. Jacques),
 20:64-68₊, July 71.

 "First African movie made by and about Africans, "
 (Kongi's Harvest), J. Bennet.   20:59-63, Sept. 71.

 "The girl who went nude for stardom, "   (Sylvette Cab-
 risseau), R. Clarke.   20:53-56, Oct. 71.

 "Hollywood's new Black beauties, "   22:37-44, Mar. 73.

 "The Black girl who plays the wife of James Bond, "
 22:35-42, May 73.
 (Gloria Hendry.)

SHOW: "Hollywood and the Black man, "   Sept. 1972, p. 61.

SOUL ILLUSTRATED: "Black screen image, "   Walter Burrell.   Feb. 1970, pp. 19-20₊.

TIME: "Power to the Peebles, "   (Melvin Van Peebles), 98:
 47, Aug. 16, 1971.

 "Black market, "   99:53, Apr. 10, 1972.

 "Cicely Tyson, "   100:58, Oct. 9, 1972.

VARIETY WEEKLY: "Jewish museums retrospective on
 Black filmmaking, back to 1916, "   Mar. 25, 1970.

 "Blaxploitationers of 1972, "   Jan. 3, 1973.
 (Summary of happenings in Black film in 1972.)

 "Violence overdone in Black capers, "   Robert B. Frederick.   Mar. 7, 1973.

 "Black actor William Marshall gives pedagogs lowdown
 on 'coon' age, "   Lee Beaupre.   Aug. 15, 1973.

WASHINGTON POST: "It's Your Thing, "   Sept. 3, 1970,
 p. C12.
 (Discussion of the soul-and-rock movie.)

"The Great White Hope, " Gary Arnold, Dec. 31, 1970,
p. C1.

"Sweetback, " Gary Arnold.   May 30, 1971, p. E3.

FILMOGRAPHY:
FEATURES BY AND ABOUT BLACKS
1904-1930

These films represent the range of motion pictures dealing with Blacks in this time span. They were included either because of their landmark value or as specimens of the films that Black filmmakers of the era were producing. Names of producers and producing companies preceded by an asterisk are white, even though subject content and all actors may be Black.

*BIOGRAPH (1904)
The Nigger in the Woodpile. Comedy in which the stereotype of the Black as lazy, stupid, childish and dishonest is presented.

*The Wooing and Wedding of a Coon (1905). All-Black cast.

BERT WILLIAMS (1914)
Darktown Jubilee. First and disastrous attempt to star a Black (Bert Williams) in a film.

*WORLD (1914)
Uncle Tom's Cabin. In this version, Sam Lucas became the first Black to portray a Black character in a film. White actors in blackface had been playing Black characters until that time.

*EPOCH (1915)
The Birth of a Nation. D. W. Griffith, director. Source: The Clansman by Thomas Dixon. The "first example of an American film showing the Negro in a villainous light. "

LINCOLN MOTION PICTURE COMPANY (1916)
Realization of a Negro's Ambition. "A two-part drama of love and adventure, pictured with a good moral, a vein of

clean comedy and beautiful settings. "

LINCOLN MOTION PICTURE COMPANY (1917)
Trooper of Troop K. "It depicts in gripping scenes the unflinching bravery of Negro troopers [of the Tenth Cavalry] under fire and how, greatly outnumbered, they sacrificed their blood and life for their country. "

COLORED AND INDIAN FILM COMPANY (1917)
Uncle Remus' First Visit to New York.

EMMETT J. SCOTT (1918)
The Birth of a Race. Produced by Emmett J. Scott in an attempt to counteract the effects of The Birth of a Nation. It was a three-hour long film, and a spectacular failure.

LINCOLN MOTION PICTURE COMPANY (1918)
The Law of Nature. "A three-reel social drama of the East and West, a virile production full of human interest and realistic western atmosphere. It deals in a gripping way of the true love of a real man and an innocent woman endangered by an ardent admirer. "

MICHEAUX PICTURES (1919)
The Homesteader.

ANDLAUER PRODUCTIONS (1921)
As the World Rolls On. Distributor: Elk Photo Plays. Cast: Jack Johnson, Blanche Thompson. Drama.

*REOL PRODUCTIONS (1921)
The Burden of Race. Drama. "At a great university, a young Negro who excels in both academic and athletic pursuits, falls in love with a white girl. "

D. W. D. FILM CORPORATION (1921)
A Child in Pawn. Melodrama.

WHITE FILM CORPORATION (1921)
A Fool's Promise. Melodrama.

BLACKBURN VELDE PRODUCTIONS (1921)
For His Mother's Sake. Five-reeler featuring Jack Johnson.

NORTH STATE FILM CORPORATION (1921)
A Giant of His Race. Drama. "A picture showing the

possibility of the individual endeavor and reward of a character of the Negro race. "

NORMAN FILM MANUFACTURING COMPANY (1921)
The Green-eyed Monster. Melodrama. "Two men,
Negroes, both in love with the same girl, work for two
different railroads.... "

MICHEAUX FILM CORPORATION (1921)
The Gunsaulus Mystery. Melodrama.

SUPREME ART PRODUCTIONS (1921)
Hearts of the Woods. Melodrama.

MICHEAUX FILM CORPORATION (1921)
The Hypocrite. Melodrama.

PROGRESS PICTURE ASSOCIATION (1921)
The Lure of a Woman. Melodrama. Distributed by
Afro-American Film Exhibitors, Inc., the "largest independ-
ent releasers and distributors of Negro photoplays. "

BEN ROY PRODUCTIONS (1921)
The Man from Texas. Western melodrama.

LINCOLN MOTION PICTURE COMPANY (1921)
A Man's Duty. The story of a young man "who, through
'cut-throat competition' for the affection of a certain young
lady, ... is made the victim of a trick by his competition,
wherein he practically brings disgrace upon himself and
family.... " Later, believing himself to be the murderer of
his rival, he leaves town and "after months of exposure, dissipation and drinking to try and, drown the effects of being a
murder, we find [him] in a far distant city, practically a
wreck on the shoals of dissipation. "

C. B. CAMPBELL STUDIO (1921)
The Negro of Today. Documentary.

MICHEAUX PICTURES (1921)
The Shadow. Melodrama.

*REOL PRODUCTIONS (1921)
The Simp. Melodrama.

E. S. AND L. COLORED FEATURE PRODUCTIONS (1921)
Square Joe. Melodrama.

*REOL PRODUCTIONS (1921)
   The Sport of the Gods. Melodrama. Source: Paul
Laurence Dunbar, The Sport of the Gods (1902). "When a
Negro Virginian is unjustly sent to prison, his family moves
to New York to escape the scorn and gossip of their neigh-
bors. "

MICHEAUX FILM CORPORATION (1921)
   Symbol of the Unconquered. Western melodrama. "After
the death of her grandfather, Evon Mason, a beautiful Negress, comes west to identify the mine claim she has been
willed. "

*REOL PRODUCTIONS (1921)
   Ties of Blood. Melodrama.

NORMAN FILM MANUFACTURING COMPANY (1922)
   The Bulldogger. Cast: Bill Pickett.

*REOL PRODUCTIONS (1922)
   The Call of His People. Cast: George Edward Brown,
Edna Morton, Mae Kemp, James Steven, Lawrence Chenault,
Mercedes Gilbert, Percy Verwayen. Melodrama. Source:
Aubrey Bowser's Man Who Would Be White. "Nelson Holmes,
a Negro passing for white ... is visited by James Graves, a
boyhood friend looking for a job. "

YOUNG PRODUCERS FILMING COMPANY (1922)
   Foolish Lives. Melodrama.

TRIO PRODUCTION COMPANY (1922)
   The Greatest Sin. Melodrama.

*REOL PRODUCTIONS (1922)
   The Jazz Hounds.

YOUNG PRODUCERS FILMING COMPANY (1922)
   The Perfect Dreamer. Melodrama.

*REOL PRODUCTIONS (1922)
   The Schemers. Melodrama. "Paul Jackson, a Negro
research chemist ... is close to success in his attempt to
develop a chemical substitute for gasoline. Juan Bronson ...
conspires ... to steal Paul's formula. "

*REOL PRODUCTIONS (1922)
   Spitfire. Melodrama. "Guy Rogers, the son of a well-

known publisher, sets out to prove his father's racist critics
wrong by putting Booker T. Washington's philosophy into
practice. "

MICHEAUX FILM CORPORATION   (1922)
     Uncle Jasper's Will.   Melodrama.

COTTON BLOSSOM FILM CORPORATION   (1922)
     Undisputed Evidence.   Melodrama.

LONE STAR MOTION PICTURE COMPANY   (1922)
     You Can't Keep a Good Man Down.

LINCOLN MOTION PICTURE COMPANY   (1923)
     By Right of Birth.   "Juanita Cooper, a pretty co-ed of a
California University ... is supposed to be of Indian ances-
try. " After a series of villainous attempts to defraud her of
her true identity and her fortune, "a happy family reunion is
celebrated and Juanita comes into the fortune and happiness
which is hers 'by right of birth'. " This feature was written
by George P. Johnson of the Lincoln Motion Picture Company.

MICHEAUX FILM CORPORATION   (1923)
     Deceit.   Melodrama.

AMERICAN COLORED FILM EXCHANGE, (distributor) (1923)
     The Devil's Match.   Jan Strasser.   Comedy-drama.

WESTERN FILM PRODUCING COMPANY   (1923)
     Flames of Wrath.   Melodrama.   "Pauline Keith, a young
Negress who works as a stenographer for William Jackson,
an unscrupulous lawyer, learns of his plan to steal a dia-
mond ... owned by Guy Braxton, a prosperous dry goods
merchant. "

MICHEAUX FILM CORPORATION   (1922)
     The Ghost of Tolston's Manor.   Melodrama.

NORMAN FILM MANUFACTURING COMPANY   (1923)
     Regeneration.   Melodrama.

MICHEAUX FILM CORPORATION   (1924)
     Birthright.   Cast: J. Homer Tutt, Evelyn Preer, Salem
Tutt Whitney, Lawrence Chenault, W. B. F. Crowell. Drama.
"A young and idealistic Negro graduate of Harvard College
goes to live in a small southern town, where he encounters
the bigotry and brutality of both races. "

NORMAN FILM MANUFACTURING COMPANY   (1924)
A Debtor to the Law.   Western melodrama.

MONARCH PRODUCTIONS   (1924)
The Flaming Crisis.   Western melodrama.   "A young
Negro newspaperman is convicted by murder on circumstantial
evidence and sentenced to prison.   He escapes and makes his
way to ... cattle country, where he falls in love with ... a
beautiful cowgirl. "

MICHEAUX FILM CORPORATION   (1924)
A Son of Satan.   Melodrama.   "Depiction of the experiences of an ordinary Negro going to a haunted house to stay
all night as the result of an argument. "

WILLIAM H. CLIFFORD PHOTOPLAY COMPANY   (1925)
The Black Boomerang.   Producer-writer William H.
Clifford.   Melodrama.

MICHEAUX FILM CORPORATION   (1925)
Body and Soul.   Cast: Paul Robeson, Julia Theresa
Russell, Mercedes Gilbert.   Melodrama.   "The story of a
man, minister of the gospel, whose habits and manner of life
are anything but that of a good man. "

MICHEAUX FILM CORPORATION   (1925)
The Brute.   Cast: Evelyn Preer, Lawrence Chenault.
Melodrama.

MICHEAUX FILM CORPORATION   (1925)
Marcus Garland.

J. W. FIFE PRODUCTIONS   (1925)
A Modern Cain.   Melodrama.   "John and Paul, Negro
twin brothers, are orphaned at an early age. ...   Grown to
manhood, they go into business together and fall in love with
the same girl.   Paul ... pushes John off a cliff.   John, who
is not killed, becomes a halfwit ... until he is cured by a
doctor.   John returns home and finds that Paul has died from
dope addiction.   He marries his sweetheart. ... "

MICHEAUX FILM CORPORATION   (1926)
The Conjure Woman.   Melodrama.

MICHEAUX FILM CORPORATION   (1926)
The Devil's Disciple.   Comedy.

COLORED MOTION PICTURE PRODUCERS OF AMERICA
(1926)
  Nine Lives. With Butterbeans and Susie.

COLORED PLAYERS FILM CORPORATION (1926)
  A Prince of His Race. Melodrama. "Tom Beuford, a
member of a good family, has fallen into disgrace through
unscrupulous associates. "

SHERMAN H. DUDLEY, JR. (1926)
  Reckless Money. Melodrama.

COLORED PLAYERS FILM CORPORATION (1926)
  Ten Nights in a Barroom. Cast: Charles Gilpin,
Lawrence Chenault, Myra Burwell, et al. Melodrama.

MICHEAUX FILM CORPORATION (1927)
  The Broken Violin. Cast: J. Homer Tutt, Ardell Dab-
ney, Alice B. Russell, Ike Paul, Daisy Foster, Gertrude
Snelson, Boots Hope, Ethel Smith, W. Hill. Melodrama.
Source: Oscar Micheaux's House of Mystery. "Lilia Cooper,
a beautiful Negress and violin prodigy, finds romance and
success despite the fact that her father is a drunkard and
her family poor. "

MICHEAUX FILM CORPORATION (1927)
  The House Behind the Cedars. Melodrama.

MGM PICTURES (1927)
  Man, Woman, and Sin. Drama.

MICHEAUX FILM CORPORATION (1927)
  The Millionaire. Melodrama. "Pelham Guitry, a Negro
soldier of fortune, goes to South America where, after 15
years of hard work, he makes his fortune ... he meets Elia
Wellington, a woman controlled by the underworld, and she
tries to trap him into marriage. Pelham defeats the forces
of crime and reforms the girl.... "

COLORED PLAYERS FILM CORPORATION (1927)
  The Scar of Shame. Drama. "Louise is beaten by her
drunken father and Alvin, a proper music student comes to
her aid. They fall in love with each other and find a few
months of married happiness.... Alvin is ashamed of
[Louise's] low birth.... Deeply hurt, Louise agrees to run
off with Spike. Alvin returns ... and accidentally wounds
Louise.... Alvin is sent to jail. Alvin breaks out of jail

and begins a new life ... falling in love with Alice....
[Louise] asks him to come back, but he refuses. She kills
herself."

MICHEAUX FILM CORPORATION (1927)
   The Spider's Web. Melodrama. "On a visit to her aunt
in a small Mississippi delta town, Norma Shepard, a young
Negro girl, is accosted on the street by Ballinger, the lech-
erous son of a white planter."

ROSEBUD FILM CORPORATION (1928)
   Absent. Supervisor-director: Harry Gant. Cast: Clar-
ence Brooks, George Reed, Virgil Owens, Rosa Lee Lincoln,
Floyd Shackelford, Clarence Williams. "A shell-shocked
Negro veteran drifts into a mining camp and is given sus-
tenance by an old miner and his daughter. He later regains
his memory in a fight and is given a fresh start by the
American Legion."

NORMAN FILM MANUFACTURING COMPANY (1928)
   Black Gold. Cast: Lawrence Corman, Kathryn Boyd.
Melodrama.

COLORED PLAYERS FILM CORPORATION (1928)
   Children of Fate. Cast: Haury Henderson, Shingzie
Howard, Lawrence Chenault, Arline Mickey. Drama.

NORMAN FILM MANUFACTURING COMPANY (1928)
   Flying Ace. May also be known as The Fighting Ace.
Melodrama.

DUNBAR FILM CORPORATION (1928)
   The Midnight Ace. Melodrama. "A young Black girl
falls in love with a master criminal, believing him to be a
good and decent man."

MICHEAUX PICTURES (1928)
   When Men Betray.

MIDNIGHT PRODUCTIONS (1928)
   Tenderfeet. Melodrama.

MICHEAUX PICTURES (1928)
   Thirty Years Later. Melodrama. "George Eldridge Van
Paul, the son of a white father and a Negro mother, is
brought up to believe that he is completely white."

MGM PICTURES   (1929)
   Hallelujah.   Drama.   Tale of a good farm boy led astray
by a temptress.

FOX FILM CORPORATION   (1929)
   Hearts in Dixie.   Comedy-drama.

MICHEAUX PICTURES   (1929)
   Wages of Sin.

MICHEAUX PICTURES   (1930)
   A Daughter of the Congo.   Melodrama.

MICHEAUX PICTURES   (1930)
   Easy Street.   Melodrama.

ARISTA FILM CORPORATION   (1930)
   Georgia Rose.   Musical comedy.

AUTHOR AND SUBJECT INDEX

This index supplies a guide to the subject listing section of the bibliography. Periodical citations are referred to by citation number. Other references are entered by page number, in parentheses, to differentiate between citation and page numbers. For example, next to the index entry "Westerns," there are the notations "(11), 429, 496." The parenthesized "11" refers to page eleven; the notations "429" and "496" refer to citations number 429 and number 496. The names of the known or cited authors of articles and other works are also listed and are capitalized throughout for easier differentiation from subject entries; names of motion pictures are underlined.

Absent (149)
Actors and Actresses (48)
  (for other citations check under names of individual actors and actresses)
Actors Equity Association 61
ADLER, RENATA (12), 237
Alexander, Bill 205, 211
ALPERT, HOLLIS 168
American Colored Film Exchange, (distributor) (146)
Anderson, Marian 336
Andlauer Productions (143)
Anna Lucasta 96
Arista Film Corporation (150)
ARNOLD, GARY 615
Arts, Sciences, and Professional Council,

(ASPC) 639, 641, 642
As the world rolls on (143)
ASPC see Arts, Sciences, and Professional Council
Association of Negro Motion Picture Producers 205

BAILEY, PEARL (15)
BART, PETER 248
Beale Street Mama 221
BEAUPRE, LEE 49, 65
BECK, MARILYN (11)
Belafonte, Harry (15), (16), 12, 16, 190, 201
Ben Roy Productions (144)
BENNETT, J. 22
BERNSTEIN, HARRY 86
Biograph movie company (142)
The birth of a nation (11), 15, 106, 252, (142), (143)

Birth of a race (143)
Birthright (146)
Black, Doris 342
Black Artists Alliance 3, 73
Black athletes (45)
Black boom (41)
The black boomerang (147)
Black capitalism 64, 176,
   177
Black cinema expo 17
Black films, filmmakers,
   filmmaking (33)
Black gold [1928] (149)
Black image (38)
Black image: men (40)
Black image: women (11)
Black like me, 263
Black musicians and
   music (47)
Blackburn Velde Produc-
   tions (143)
Blacks, films, and politics
   see Politics
Blacks, films, and social
   tensions see Racism
Blount, Mildred 133
Body and soul [1925] (147)
BOGLE, DONALD (13), 4,
   7
"Bojangles" see Robinson,
   Bill
BOND, FREDERICK (13)
Bourne, St. Clair 213
The broken violin (148)
Bronze buckaroo (11)
Brown, Jim 178
The brute (147)
Buck and the preacher 278,
   287
The bulldogger (145)
Burden of race (143)
BURG, ROBERT 394
BURKE, VINCENT T. 139
BURRELL, WALTER 91,
   229, 258
By right of birth (146)

C. A. B. see Coalition Against
   Blaxploitation
Call of duty 211
The call of his people (145)
CAMERON, EARL 38
C. B. Campbell Studio (144)
Carroll, Diahann (16)
Carver, Dr. George Wash-
   ington 121
Cash, Rosalind 258
Central Casting Corporation
   69
Chamba Productions, Inc.,
   213
CHAMPLIN, CHARLES 244
Child in pawn (143)
Children of fate (149)
Civil rights (67)
William H. Clifford Photo-
   play Company (147)
Coalition Against Blaxploita-
   tion 3
Cole, Nat 'King' 330, 338
Colored and Indian Film
   Company (143)
Colored Motion Picture Pro-
   ducers of America (148)
Colored Players Film Corp-
   oration 214, (148), (149)
Columbia Pictures 71, 72
Comments and criticism (42)
COMPO see Council of Mo-
   tion Picture Organizations
The conjure woman (147)
Cool breeze 278, 287
Cool world 41, 168, 263
Cosby, Bill 227
Cotton Blossom Corporation
   (146)
COUCH, WILLIAM, JR. 243
Council of Motion Picture
   Organizations 100
CRIPPS, THOMAS R. 12,
   232
CRIST, JUDITH (11)
Crouch, William 194
CROWTHER, BOSLEY 40

CRUSE, HAROLD (11)

D. W. D. Film Corporation
  (143)
Dandridge, Dorothy (15),
  314
Darktown jubilee (142)
Daughter of the Congo (150)
Davis, Angela 212
Davis, Ossie (15), 117
DAVIS, PATRICIA E. 643,
  647
DE ANDA, PETER 304
A debtor to the law (147)
Deceit (146)
DEE, RUBY (15), 262
DELEIHBUR, DON 130
DENIS, PAUL 43
The devil's disciple (147)
The devil's match (146)
Dirty Gertie from Harlem
  USA 221
Dobson, Tamara 257
DU BOIS, W. E. B. 6
Dunbar Film Corporation
  (149)

E. S. and L. Colored
  Feature Productions (144)
Easy street (150)
Ellington, Duke 329
ELLIS, ROBERT 85, 98,
  105
Embassy Pictures 195
The Emperor Jones (13)
Epoch Movie Company (142)
Equal Employment Oppor-
  tunity Commission 138

Falana, Lola 259
FAY, STEPHEN 233
FEATHER, LEONARD 289
FERDERBER, SKIP 344
FESSIER, MICHAEL, JR. 78

J. W. Fife Productions (147)
Film and Black athletes (45)
Fitzgerald, Ella 337
Flames of wrath (146)
The flaming crisis (147)
Flying ace (149)
Foolish lives (145)
Fool's promise (143)
For his mother's sake (143)
FORD, NICK AARON 516
Franklin, Wendell 175, 191
FREDERICK, ROBERT B.
  294, 310

GAREY, DORIS B. 515
GARFIELD, JOHN 94
Georgia, Georgia 278
Georgia Rose (150)
The ghost of Tolston's
  manor (146)
Giant of his race (143)
GIPSON, GERTRUDE 282
Goldberg, Jack and Bert
  186, 221
GOODMAN, GEORGE 347
The greatest sin (145)
Greaves, William 180, 226
GREEN, LARRY 84
GREEN, THEOPHILUS 253
Green-eyed monster (144)
Greene, Joe 145
Grier, Pam 257
Griffin, Junius 271
Griffith, D. W. (11)
Guess who's coming to
  dinner 422
Gunn, Bill 294
Gunsaulus mystery (144)

Hallelujah (150)
HALLIBURTON, CECIL D.
  235
Hairston, Jester 334
HANDSAKER, GENE 113
Handy, W. C. 338

HARDWICK, LEON H.
  118, 246
Harlem rides the range
  (11)
HARMON, SIDNEY 96
HARTUNG, PHILIP T. 154
Hearts in Dixie (150)
Hearts of the woods (144)
Hendry, Gloria 257
HESTON, CHARLTON 60
Highest tradition 211
History of Blacks in
  films (18)
Holly, Floyd 69
Hollywood (23)
Home of the brave 9, 51,
  112, 156
Homesteader 143
HORTON, LUCI 257
House behind the cedars
  (148)
HULL, BOB 70
HUMPHREY, HAL 227
HUNT, MARSHA 80
HUNTER, ROBERT G. 83
Hypocrite (144)

IATSE see International
  Alliance of Theatrical
  Stage Employes
Illinois Chamber of Com-
  merce 67
Image see Black image
Imrie, Kathy 259
Indepth Productions 207
International Alliance of
  Theatrical Stage Employes
  78, 97
Interracialism in films
  (31), 275, 278, 309
Intruder in the dust 51
ISAACS, EDITH J. (14), 10

Jackson, Jesse 196
Jackson, Mahalia 333

The jazz hounds (145)
JENKINS, W. 405
JEROME, V. J. (14), 640
Joe Louis Story 316
JOHNSON, ALBERT 36, 275
Jones, Ike 195
JONES, ROBERT 95

KAGAN, NORMAN 2
KAUFMAN, DAVE 135
Kaufmann, Stanley 307
KAY, CHARLOTTE 387
Kelly, Paula 259, 282
KILLENS, JOHN OLIVER
  (12)
King, Rev. Martin Luther
  198, 244
KING, WOODIE JR. 52
KISTLER, ROBERT 77
Kitzmiller, John 55
KNAPP, DAN 63
KNIGHT, ARTHUR 42
KRONENBERGER, LOUIS 93
Ku Klux Klan 646

LANDRY, ROBERT J. 234
Law of nature (143)
LAWSON, JOHN H. (11), 641
LEAB, D. J. 5
Lee, Canada 12, 319
Legend of nigger Charley 287
LEITES, NATHAN 309
Lincoln Motion Picture
  Company (142), (143), 197,
  214
LOBSENZ, ALLEN C. 117
Lone Star Motion Picture
  Company (146)
Lost boundaries (10), 9, 155
Lure of a woman (144)

McGee, Vonetta 257, 259
McManus, John T. 93
Man from Texas (144)

Man, woman and sin (148)
A man's duty (144)
MAPP, EDWARD (14), 23
Marcus Garland (147)
Marshall, George 72
MASON, CLIFFORD 426
MATTOX, MICHAEL 213
Mercer, Mae 259
Metro-Goldwyn-Mayer 116,
    (148), (150)
Micheaux Pictures (143),
    (144), (145), (146), (147),
    (148), (149), (150), 192,
    197, 214
The midnight ace (149)
Midnight Productions (149)
MILLER, LOREN (12),
    252, 292
The millionaire (148)
MITCHELL, LOFTEN (14)
Mister Washington goes to
    town 284
A modern Cain (147)
Monarch Productions (147)
Moore, Lisa 259
MOORE, WALTER 31
MOORING, WILLIAM 305
MORRISON, ALLAN 11
MOSS, CARLTON 35
Movies (57) (for other
    citations check under
    names of individual movies)
Mulattoes 130, 162
MURPHY, A. D. 131
MURRAY, JAMES P. 19
Music and musicians (47)

NAACP 88, 97, 107, 110,
    113, 127
Nash, Johnny 339
NCI 108
NCOMP 109
Negro Critics Circle 112
Negro of today (144)
NEWSOM, JIM 108
Nicholas, Denise 259

Nigger in the woodpile (142)
Nine lives (148)
No way out 105
NOBLE, PETER (14)
Norman Film Manufacturing
    Company (144), (145),
    (146), (147), (149)
Norman, Maidie 312, 630
North State Film Corpora-
    tion (143)
Nothing but a man 168

OLSON, DALE 204
Our gang 344, 575

Pace, Judy 259, 282
Parks, Gordon 140, 187,
    188, 189
Patch of blue 422
PATTERSON, LINDSAY (15),
    251, 291
Payne, Freda 259
PENNINGTON, RON 273
The perfect dreamer (145)
PETERS, BROCK 65, 134
Peters, Thomas A. 207
Pinky 9, 51
Poitier, Sidney (12), (16),
    8, 41, 65, 234, 236
Politics (66)
PRELUTSKY, BURT 236
A prince of his race (148)
Progress Picture Associa-
    tion (144)
PUSH 64, 123

Racism (67)
Realization of a Negro's
    ambition (142)
Reckless money (148)
Regeneration (146)
Reol Productions (143),
    (144), (145)
Revue - Universal Pictures
    116

Rich, Ron 142
RILEY, CLAYTON 283
RINGE, PAUL 82
Roberts, Davis 113
Roberson, Paul (16)
Robinson, Bill "Bo-
  jangles" (16), 12
ROBINSON, L. 415
Robson, Mark 85
Rosebud Film Corpora-
  tion (149)
Ross, Diana 259
ROTH, HENRY 332

SANDERS, CHARLES 423,
  439, 442
Sands, Diana 259
Scar of shame (148)
Schapiro, Sue 220
The schemers (145)
Scott, Emmett J. (143)
Screen Directors Guild 174
SEIDENBAUM, ART 249
SELZNICK, DAVID O. 115
The shadow (144)
The simp (144)
SMALLWOOD, WILLIAM
  133
Smith, Leonard 215
A son of satan (147)
Soul soldier 287
The spider's web (149)
Spitfire (145)
Splendora Film Corporation
  206
Sport of the gods (145)
Spying the spy (12)
Square Joe (144)
Stepin Fetchit 236, 314
Stereotypes, Black see
  Black image
Story of a three-day pass
  216
STRICK, ANNE 122
Supreme Art Productions
  (144)

Sweet Sweetback's baad-
  assss song (12), (71)
Sykes, Brenda 259
Symbol of the unconquered
  (145)

Ten nights in a barroom
  (148)
Tenderfeet (149)
Thirty years later (149)
THOMPSON, C. A. 422
Thompson, True 221
Ties of blood (145)
TOPPIN, EDGAR A. (16)
Trio Production Company
  (145)
Trooper of Troop K (143)
TRUMBO, DALTON 231
Tubbs, Vincent 44, 137
TUSHER, WILL 64, 177,
  230
Twentieth Century Fox Pic-
  tures 146
Tyson, Cicely 259

Uncle Jasper's will (146)
Uncle Remus' first visit to
  New York (143)
Uncle Tom's cabin (142)
Undisputed evidence (146)

Valenti, Jack 140
Van Peebles, Melvin 174,
  208, 216, 223

Wages of sin (150)
Ware, Margaret 259
Warner Pictures 127, 140
Washington, Hazel 133
Waters, Ethel (16), 314
WEALES, GERALD 51
WEIL, PEGGY 125
WEISMAN, AL 155

WELKER, ROBERT   12
WESTERBECK, COLIN L.
   JR.   278
Western Film Producing
   Company (146)
WESTERNS (11), 429, 496
When men betray   (149)
White Film Corporation (143)
WHITE, WALTER 245
WILKINS, ROY 15, 111
Williams, Bert (15), (16),
   (142)
WOLFENSTEIN, MARTHA
   309
WOOD, COLLETTE 178
Wooing and wedding of a
   coon (142)
World Movie Company (142)
WYATT, EUPHEMIA V. R.
   517

YAMADA, GEORGE   241
You can't keep a good man
   down (146)
YOUNG, A. S. "DOC" 44,
   54, 132, 367
Young, Whitney 225
Young Producers Filming
   Company (145)

Zanuck, Darryl 146
ZITO, STEPHEN (13), 214